Riding Grace

A Triumph of the Soul

Vita at three

Vita was Alissa Lukara's birth name.
She legally changed it to Alissa Lukara in 2000.

Riding Grace

A Triumph of the Soul

ALISSA LUKARA

SILVER LIGHT
PUBLICATIONS

SILVER LIGHT
PUBLICATIONS

Silver Light Publications
2305 C Ashland Street #426
Ashland, Oregon 97520
www.silverlightpub.com

First Edition
♻ Printed in Canada on 100% postconsumer waste recycled paper. A proud member of the Green Press Initiative.

Distributed to the trade by Publishers Group West and Publishers Group Worldwide

Cover design by Nita Ybarra
Interior design by Confluence Book Services

Publisher's Cataloging-in-Publication
(Provided by Quality Books, Inc.)

Lukara, Alissa.
    Riding grace: a triumph of the soul / by Alissa
Lukara.
    p. cm.
    LCCN 2006920771
    ISBN 0-9744890-3-4

    1. Lukara, Alissa. 2. Incest victims--United States
--Biography. 3. Adult child sexual abuse victims--
United States--Biography. 4. Chronic fatigue syndrome--
Patients--Biography. 5. Self-actualization (Psychology)
--Religious aspects. 6. Spiritual life. I. Title.

HV6570.7.L85 2007   362.76'4'092
            QBI06-600030

Table of Contents

To the children

Prologue

Jonah tells me I should have been an ax murderer, what with my Lizzie-Borden-in-the-making kind of childhood. "Instead," he says, "you're a miracle. You make all discussion about whether genetics or environment determine a person's character moronic and irrelevant."

If you had become an ax murderer, he says, the psychologists who studied your case would simply "tsk" their tongues, shake their heads and conclude, "Well, what else could she have been? Fascist dictator. Raging psychotic. Check one or all of the above."

"Add what's occurred in these last years, and you should at least be a broken, embittered human being. Instead," Jonah says, "you're this loving, compassionate, wise, powerful woman. You've not only endured a lot, but you're thriving. Who you are clearly isn't about genetics or environment; it's about the evolution of your soul."

Now, granted, Jonah is a bit over the top when it comes to going on about my attributes. He is my life partner, after all, and loves me more than I thought it possible for another human to love anyone, let alone me.

But he is right. I am a miracle, or maybe I should say, I'm a person to whom miracles happen regularly—a miracle magnet. I've experienced Lazarus-rising-from-the-dead kinds of miracles, help-when-all-seems-lost miracles, and other varieties, too. Some come like shock waves, reverberating through my whole being. Others drift by like a gentle breeze, so imperceptibly glancing across my face that I almost miss them. At times, I'm looking for them. Often, they're looking for me. I could be a poster child for miracles, I've experienced so many.

I'm not so deluded, however, as to think they occur to me because I'm somebody special. I happen to believe that miracles are available to everyone daily—including the ax murderers. We just have to keep our eyes and heart open in order to see them, have faith that they exist and invite them into our lives without question when they appear.

We need to do that even when miracles don't look like what we think they should, or they're not the ones we asked for, or they aren't certified by the Catholic Church. Even when we don't think we're good enough to deserve them, or we think that surely, we've had our quota of miracles for this lifetime.

All I know is that without them, without the infusion of grace and life force that accompanies them, I wouldn't be alive or functional. Worse yet—I might actually have ended up as one of those other possibilities for my future that Jonah mentioned.

I didn't always know this. I didn't know that I could actually feel so much aliveness, gratitude, joy, and love—or that I would ever experience so much choice in my life, because Jonah is right about something else, too. He's right when he says I've gone through a lot. I'm not whining. This isn't a "woe is me" sort of tale. In fact, while I don't always live up to it, I'm a big proponent of the anonymous quote: "Pain is inevitable, but suffering is optional."

But if I were an outsider looking in on my life, I'd say, "Gee, no way I could survive that." Yet I did survive, and more than that, I learned to choose life fully. Not only the good and fun parts, but all of it. I shock even myself when I say that I tenderly hold a space inside me where I bless each moment, person, tear, and smile. Each trial honed me with such exquisite precision to know, accept and offer the gift of my life, the gift of me.

Both miracles—and horrors—have served as guideposts and gateways on a journey that led me again and again deep into the underworld of the ancient goddesses, Inanna and Persephone, my spirit sisters. Slowly, with the help of many allies, I clawed and dug and was lifted out repeatedly to live in the land of kaleidoscopic seasons and shades of light. Here, now, I learn to breathe life into a new kind of power in myself. At its heart, this power centers on acceptance of what seems unacceptable, forgiveness of what seems unforgivable, love, compassion, healing, freedom, peace, connection, respect for all life and co-creation with Great Spirit.

I dedicate this story to the child that I was—in particular to the 3-year-old, the 7-year-old, and the 15-year-old of me. I dedicate it to all the children who are and were and will be. The child that was me was saved over and over again by the stories that she read, that were read to her, that became part of her and coursed through her veins like lifeblood. She longed to the depth of her soul to live to tell stories that would touch others, but didn't dare hope she ever could. Her own voice was silenced so completely, turned inward, a giant cork stuck down her throat. I give you your voice back, my sweet one. I invite you to speak here as you wish in the telling of this tale, to speak your own stories in your own way. Be as loud as you want.

So—"fasten your seat belts. It's going to be a bumpy night," as Bette Davis says in *All About Eve*. But I promise you up front: We do find the Holy Grail. Its liquid heals my parched throat and rekindles the fires of my thirst. The thing is: There is no ending here, happy or otherwise.

Remembering

2 a.m., June 14, 1998

Let's get one thing straight. I don't want to write this book. I've been running away from writing it for years. My own story. I'm afraid to write it. Almost as afraid as I was when it happened. But I can't run away anymore. Not because of any high and mighty reason, but simply because the pain of not writing it has grown bigger than the pain of writing it.

And while I am afraid that if I write it, I will be killed, ostracized, shunned, and hated—not necessarily in that order. While I am afraid that in letting go of the controls I have held onto for so long, I will become the very insanity about which I write. I find myself face to face with the knowing that the energy I'm using not to write it has turned against me and is killing me slowly. Draining life force. This book has become a matter of life and death for me—if not a physical death, then the death of the very spirit I worked so hard to save all these years. Controlling myself and my words isn't working any more. Not that it ever did.

What I also realize is that as fast as I have been finding ways to free myself, to write and let my voice out, my beautiful ego has been coming up with ever more clever ways to shut me up again. To protect me. All in the name of keeping me safe.

Ego, let me tell you here and now, I love you very much. I appreciate your attempts and the good job you've done in helping me survive. I'm not looking to put you out of a job, but you've got to be exhausted. It can't be much fun having to be on red alert and resisting all the time. So, I'd like to give you a nice long vacation and a new job title for when you return. How about "Passion Truth Promoter?"

Times have changed, dear ego. Now, our safety doesn't lie in hiding. It's in telling the truth.

So tonight. This very night before God, I commit myself to stop running, to stop bargaining with God about what else I might write about—and to tell this story. All of it that needs to be told. For while the story may seem to be a simple one of good and evil, with me being one of the wronged good guys, done to instead of doing, it's not so straightforward as all that. It's a story about the need for healing, not only for the innocents, but for those who have been doing the doing, too. It's a story that leaps, eyes open, into that space beyond good and evil and stokes the fires of divine perspective, which burn away blame and shame.

Let's get one more thing straight. Writing this book is the only choice I can make right now that leads me back to life. Life is the meaning of Vita, the name given to me at birth by my father. This is my choice.

⁓

I write these words in my journal at two a.m. Twelve hours later, I sit in a workshop led by two healers in a Southern Oregon Grange building. In the space of a few minutes, I experience a complete, spontaneous physical healing of the Chronic Fatigue Syndrome that has plagued me for 12 years. It's hard even for me to ignore that this is a pretty large exclamation point to my decision to write this book. And so I begin.

⁓

May 1986

Once I was a do-er. I did things. I worked. I wrote. I socialized. I interacted. I thought. I hiked. I made love. I read. I traveled.

I went to cultural events. I had goals and dreams—most of which involved doing.

I loved to dance. Freeform dance. My body actually moved me, and I followed the energy as it spun around and wove its web of fluid, jerky all-encompassing motion. It was more than dancing really. It was my soul expressing itself, giving my body a way to connect with its life force and rhythm. Stories would emerge and tell themselves in its movements. I loved my body—marveled at how all its organs and cells and bones and blood and skin coalesced to give me a form for personal expression and manifestation on this earth. I loved life. I loved living actively in my body.

But that's all gone now. The body I counted on, took for granted as my partner in doing, is no longer cooperating. The body I counted on has been violated by a chronic illness. First diagnosed as Epstein-Barre virus, it would later come to be recognized as Chronic Fatigue Syndrome (CFS), also known as Chronic Fatigue Immune and Dysfunction Syndrome, an illness impacting nearly one million people and defined by the US Centers for Disease Control and Prevention.

Now, I am a be-er instead of a do-er. For the most part, I live my life in what I come to call the gray zone, existence at the level of monochrome. The starring cast of my particular black-and-white movie consists of several pages worth of CFS symptoms.

Top billing goes to fatigue. Where healthy people's fatigue is a crack in the sidewalk, CFS fatigue is the Grand Canyon. A famous CFS doctor says it's like comparing a wind gust to a hurricane.

A master at its craft, fatigue's performance in my body is loaded with nuance. Besides a one-note exhaustion, it enacts liver fatigue, which comes with a touch of bloating, crankiness, depression, flu-like aches, and a sapping of my will.

A portrayal of lack-of-REM-sleep fatigue is tinged with restlessness. It's like a high-strung, burned-out racehorse with broken legs.

Night-of-the-Living-Dead fatigue turns me into a zombie. Here, all I do is lie quietly, unable to talk, enshrouded in dull pain.

One-two-punch fatigue knocks me down fast and hard. It strikes when I push beyond the little energy I have and step off the cliff into the space where reserve energy used to catch my fall. Now, I plummet straight into the canyon floor.

The second star is loss of concentration, its role triggered by severe allergies and brain lesions that impair the electrical firing across neurological synapses. Daily, it robs me of the capacity to read anything as complex as literature, write, think, reason much, or work. It's also a master of surprise. Imagine me in the middle of a conversation with my husband Jonah suddenly unable to comprehend him. Mind out of order, I only know that I used to know but no longer do. At times this scene is accented with a special flourish of anger and tears of frustration.

With regularity, these two main stars pose questions that physically healthy people never even fathom. "With the energy and concentration I have to do one thing today, do I fix dinner, wash my hair, make love to my husband, or sit in the park for an hour?" Or, "I'd like to see friends for a couple hours. Do I have the two full days I need to prepare for the visit—a full day of rest beforehand so I can do it, plus a full day afterward to recover?"

Dizziness and memory loss play major roles, too—real scene-stealers. Dizziness often accompanies low blood sugar. Without warning, I can't stand or talk anymore. When Jonah is near, he shows how well he can play a character that "goes into emergency." Anxiously, with great concern, he guides me to a place to lie down and gets me something to eat to raise my blood sugar.

Memory loss often embellishes loss of concentration with an inability to remember names of things or what I did the day or hour before. It usually results in a vacant stare, which prompts Jonah to ask, "Are you still here? Do you need to rest?"

There are the supporting characters, too. Joint and muscle aches. Intermittent sore throats and swollen glands. Sleep disturbances. Night sweats. Environmental and food sensitivities. Digestive problems. Vision distortions. Liver pains. Sporadic depression and grief. Inability to handle the heightened stimulation of fluorescent lights, the smells of grocery and department stores, sitting close to a movie screen, or being near electrical appliances. These are a few ways CFS impacts every organ or system in my body.

A well-known CFS specialist will write that people with this illness experience every day what cancer and AIDS patients who are dying experience three months before their deaths. Years later, I will meet a PhD author and researcher specializing in healing and the power of visualization and prayer on healing. At the time, she was facing cancer herself. She will say, "Chronic Fatigue Syndrome. Now there's a challenge. Healing cancer is a piece of cake in comparison."

Little do I know that I am about to encounter something in my life that will, for a time, make the CFS itself look like a piece of cake.

May 5, 1986

Philippe is a lean, blond, attractive man in his mid-thirties, medium height, with a gentle smile. His small house sits near an entrance to Topanga Canyon State Park outside Los Angeles. The healing room that he uses to do his laying on of hands energy healing work is set up so that it looks out onto the sunlit park through sliding glass doors. On one peach-colored wall hangs a painting of a Native American elder surrounded by an eagle, a wolf, a mountain lion, and a bear. Next to it is a dream catcher, a wooden circle with a pattern of interlaced string inside and feathers hanging from the bottom. Dream catchers supposedly deflect nightmares and negativity, allowing positive dreams to pass through. Rose quartz crystals and chunks of amethyst line the windowsills.

Philippe has been referred to me by my holistic MD, Jim, to help with the CFS. Never having had an energy healing, I'm moving outside my comfort zone. But I'm open to the concept, believe in the possibility of miraculous and longer term healings using this method. Frankly, I'm also desperate. After six months, I'm still too ill to walk a block without support or drive myself the 45 minutes it takes to get to Topanga from Jonah's and my West Hollywood apartment. So far, none of the medicinal, herbal or nutritional remedies I've tried has helped me get my life back.

Philippe explains his process. "As I see it, healers are channels for energy which you direct toward your own highest healing. Universal healing energy passes through me to you and clears energy blockages. As energy flows freely in each of your chakras, the energy centers of the body, your own body can take over and heal itself."

He notes that I might experience different sensations—warmth, rushes of energy, shaking—or feel a variety of emotions. "In our bodies, we hold the memories of all the experiences and emotions we've never released," he says. "If any come up, let me know. We can explore them."

After removing my shoes and jewelry, I lie face up on a massage table, covered with a soft lavender blanket. Gently placing his hands on different areas of my body, Philippe begins. Warmth and energy run up and down my legs, arms, and torso, creating a sense of well being. Slowly, I drift into a meditative state.

I feel him press down harder on my upper abdomen at the third chakra, which is associated with personal power and will. And the world as I have known it begins to crack. An abrupt mudslide of emotion rips me from my bearings like a house falling down a cliff during a California rainstorm. The adult Vita is gone, her replacement, a gasping, whimpering child. Her forehead tenses. She shakes uncontrollably. She feels more terror than she has ever known it was possible to feel. This is the kind of fright you could die from. I can barely spit out the words, "I'm scared, I'm scared," over and over.

"How old are you?" Philippe asks.

"Three." My answer comes independent of any thought.

"What's happening?"

"My father...He's hitting me."

"Why?"

"I don't know. He says, I've been bad...I don't know what I've done, what I could have possibly done to deserve this... He's hitting me. I'm scared..."

"What's he saying?"

"You're bad, Vita."

"Say it again."

"You're bad."

"And again."

"You're bad."

"What else?"

"You're evil." Philippe asks me to repeat each thing I hear three times. Each word strikes me as painfully as my father's fists.

"You deserve this. You're a slut."

Slut? Here, for the first time through the terror, a space opens. A thought slips into my mind. *Why is my father calling me a slut when I'm only three years old?*

Then, as my father, I hear myself saying, "If you tell your mother, I'll kill you both. I'll slice you both up into little pieces."

Another thought. *Why is it such a big deal that I tell my mother? She already knows that my father beats me. What difference would it make?*

Philippe's voice pulls me back. "How are you responding?"

"I'm crying, afraid for my life...terrified...helpless...overwhelmed by this huge, raging out of control man."

"How would you like to respond? Say it three times."

"Stop it."

"Louder."

"Stop it," I scream. "Stop it. Stop hurting me. Get off of me."

Again, I momentarily question why I chose this last phrase.

"I'm good. I don't deserve this. I hate you. I want to hurt you."

Rage and hurt and shame and pain sweep over me and carry me. I'm amazed at how much energy I have. But gradually, I've expended all I can.

When Philippe asks me if I've finished, I say yes, but that I don't feel like I've gotten to all of it. There's something more to come.

After the session, my energy level has improved. I am thrilled. "I had no idea I still had so much rage at my father," I tell Philippe. "I thought I'd worked it out in past therapy."

I relate that I first encountered anger at my father a few years earlier. I'd been in Gestalt therapy in New York City, where I used to live. For three years, in weekly private and group sessions, I looked at the extent of my father's physical and emotional abusiveness and tapped the rage, sadness, and other emotions I had repressed about it. I'm surprised my anger is coming up so strongly again.

Wanting to explore what feels incomplete, I set up an appointment for the following week.

⌒

As Jonah drives us home, I tell him about my experience. "How weird that your father called you a slut," he says.

"I thought so, too."

"You don't think he sexually molested you, do you?" he asks.

My heart begins to pound. "No way," I answer without taking a breath, without pausing to let Jonah's words register. "I mean, he already did so much. But I can't believe he did that, too. I've always said my sexuality was one part of my life my father didn't mess up. Being from Europe, he and my mother had an open attitude about it. Do you really think he molested me?"

"I don't know. No. Probably not. What you experienced him saying doesn't quite make sense. That's all."

As we head down the Pacific Coast Highway toward Sunset Boulevard, the sun glints off the ocean waves and shines through the window, warming my face and chest. I mull the words in my mind. Sexual molestation. Watching media coverage over the last year about recovering repressed memories of incest, I had actually considered whether I too might have been sexually abused. But I'd dismissed the possibility, didn't believe I could repress something that horrendous.

I close my eyes to take a nap, but I can't sleep. My mind is racing. Wanting to move away from the idea of sexual abuse, it grabs onto thought after thought of the abuse I do remember experiencing by the time I was three years old—or was told by my parents had happened. Thoughts like my mother admitting that my father bullied her into leaving me alone from the time I was six weeks old so that they could go out for the evening. When I was six months old, I pulled myself up the railings of the crib and fell out. I screamed so loudly that the neighbors broke in and found me on the floor.

The thought of my father beating me with a belt, extending those beatings if I dared to cry in response. "I was teaching you to hide emotions," my father said years later. "They only get you in trouble."

The memory of the terror. Never knowing what would trigger his violence, because it rarely resulted from my actually misbehaving. No matter how I was, what I did or said, I could not stop it.

The remembrance of his verbal rages. A past heavyweight boxer, he'd scream at me and simultaneously pound the institution green walls of our tiny one-bedroom apartment so hard that they cracked.

The recollection of his locking me in the closet after his physical and verbal rages, sometimes for hours. I remember that closet. It was the only one in our apartment in Cleveland, Ohio, where I spent the first years of my childhood. I remember sitting completely still and silent amongst the shoes on the wood floor. Only a glimmer of light shone through the door cracks. Enveloped in darkness, burying tears and rage, I knew that if I made a sound, my father would beat me again. The air was thick and musty and hot. I felt like I was breathing bricks into my lungs. To remind myself that I existed, I ran my fingers across my face, mouth, and nose.

I remember reaching up to touch one of my mother's dresses, neatly sandwiched between my father's garments and my own. I held its soft fabric against my cheek. I breathed in the sweet flower smell of her. It made me feel safer somehow, protected.

There, in the dark, it was as if she put her arms around me and shielded me from my father in a way that, out in the light of day, she did not.

Physical and verbal abuse, yes. No question, I think to myself once again back in the present in Los Angeles. Giving up on the nap, I open my eyes to the bright sun, breathe in the scent of car exhaust intermingled with ocean air. *But it's a long leap off a precipice and across a canyon full of jagged rocks to move from the abuse I remember to incest.*

———

As the car turns away from the ocean onto Sunset Boulevard, a small faint voice inside me suggests, "Imagine for a moment that your father did molest you. Just for a moment."

Okay, I think, releasing resistance. *What harm could come from that? Just for a moment.* I let my defenses down, let go the *No. No. No. Impossible. Not me. Not my father. Too awful.* And say, *Suppose he did sexually molest me. Okay. He did.* I take a deep breath.

At that instant, a tsunami hits my psyche. It sweeps away my entire past as I have known it, like it never existed. I'm right back in the terror I felt while lying on Philippe's healing table. I *am* the terror. It's all I am, all I ever have been and all I ever will be. And more. One feeling after another seizes and overpowers me. I no longer simply feel. I am shame. I am pain. I am guilt. I am anger.

On the way to Philippe's, Jonah had mentioned that he was inexplicably nervous. "All day I've felt shaky, like something might happen that will irrevocably change things," Jonah had said. "It's weird. I hope we don't have a major earthquake."

Well, it turns out that I am the earthquake, 7.9 on the Richter scale—foundations crumbling, shattering, turning to liquid quicksand. I sink sink sink unable to grab hold of anything or anyone. No, I say to myself, trying to stop what's happening—as if I still have a chance to make another choice in the matter. *Enough. No more,* I say, trying to calm and still the rocking and shaking and sinking going on. But the voice is too late. The undammed feelings give way to a flood of images now.

They come like full force aftershocks, one wave after another. Flashing graphic pictures of child porn, and the star is me.

My father and I are in the shower. He is fondling my genitals and rubbing his penis on my back.

No.

I lie face down on the bed, and he sticks his finger up me.

No.

I sit in his lap naked, and he kisses me all over my face and chest.

No, I say. *Not possible*, I say. But I know. It is.

It did happen. As our silver blue Honda Accord hatchback winds its way through Beverly Hills, I know it in every part of me. Mansions, bastions of order and seeming sanity with their perfectly landscaped grounds and perfectly trimmed shrubs and trees, stand lined up to my right and left. They and their inhabitants are unaware that a quake, a federal disaster area in the making, is moving through their midst.

I tell Jonah. "I'm either remembering real events or having a psychotic break right here in the car. I can't believe that I was sexually molested. But I do believe it. I'm beginning to, at least. Do you think I'm crazy? Do I seem crazy?"

I will ask Jonah this question at least 100 times over the next days.

"You don't seem crazy," he answers again and again. "I'm afraid that you're perfectly sane. *This* must be what was making me nervous earlier."

"But look at everything I've worked on in therapy over the years. All the anger I've released," I say. "How could I have explored myself so closely, yet blocked this out?"

"Don't be so hard on yourself," Jonah says. "This is pretty big stuff. The way I see it, you weren't ready. And now you are. You're remembering it now, because you're strong enough to handle it."

Over the next days, the once understandable, known land-scapes of my life, the familiar places, the paths leading some-where disappear. They give way to a land of pitch-black caverns of primal screams, ocean riptides of tears, frenzied cyclones of hate and vengefulness, avalanches of shame, barren valleys of loss, searing forest fires of terror, erupting volcanoes of pain. There is no shelter here. Only darkness. Fully exposed to all elements, I have lost what I thought was my reality forever.

Each time the feelings are as I experienced them in the car. When I scream, I become screaming. When I cry, I become crying. Screaming screams me. Crying cries me, like deep rolling tidal waves. Sometimes, I shake uncontrollably.

I can't even reach out to where Jonah is. In the distance, he stands arms extended, calling to me. I try to reach back, to take the hands that want to pull me to safety. But I can't. I can only allow him to witness. It does help to know that he is there, some sort of reference point to which I attempt to return. It helps that he can see where I am, too. But I am buried alive. I have to scratch my own way out.

My hope is that I have gone mad, entered some sort of psychotic hallucination. But I have not. I have simply remembered the truth.

In those first days, pinned under the debris of flashbacks, pieces of a past finally unearthed and exposed, I try to grab onto something tangible in this vast unknown.

I decide to call Sonia, a friend I know who was molested. Sonia also blocked out her molestation until adulthood. I recall the first time she told me her story, two years earlier. Sonia and I had spent the afternoon up on Mount Tamalpais in Marin County outside San Francisco. The sumptuous landscape rolled out before us, lushly green from winter rains. In the distance, the ocean shimmered in the sun.

Amidst that natural beauty, she recounted that starting when she was three years old, her father had molested her for years. Her mother had condoned it. Afterward, I cried for the better part of 24 hours, at the horror of it, I thought. I hadn't realized incest could start at such a young age.

"I know it's terrible, but why are you having such a huge reaction?" Jonah asked me back then.

"How could I not," I answered defensively. "I'm empathizing. I'm aghast at the evil people do to each other. Besides, Sonia is the first person who ever talked to me about incest."

I thought my reaction was normal, that Jonah didn't react as strongly because he wasn't a woman, couldn't understand what it was like to grow up with the constant threat of sexual violation.

Now, I sit at my desk in our second bedroom, which doubled as my office before I came down with CFS. The desk, devoid of any remnants of my work, has a few knickknacks on it—a glass dragon holding a crystal ball, a ceramic red heart with rainbow wings, a beach rock, a statue of a white horse, an animal ally that helps me access my creativity. The Venetian blinds on the street level window remain closed.

I dial Sonia's number. I want to know what triggered her memory, how she survived remembering. I want corroboration that what's happening to me happened to someone else. I want to know it isn't my fault. I don't deserve it. I'm not crazy.

"No, you're not crazy," says Sonia. "At first, I thought I was, too. Everything you're experiencing is normal for an incest survivor."

I call the hotline at an organization called Women Helping Women. "You're not crazy," says the woman who answers. "Your reactions are typical." She gives me the names of two therapists who specialize in sexual abuse.

I realize that besides the work with Philippe, I also need support from someone who knows facts about incest and its perpetrators. I call and set up an appointment for the next day with one of her recommendations, a therapist named Sherry.

Sherry's Westwood office is white. White pictureless walls. White desk. White director's chair for her. White loveseat and pillows for me. The color comes in accents, tiny bursts—a green fern and Swedish ivy hanging by the window, a vase of fresh cut pastel-colored flowers, stuffed animals set out for clients to use.

Tall and thin, with curly brown chin length hair, Sherry wears casual clothes and little make up. She works with both adult and child incest survivors, specializes in this area, she explains, because when she was 13, she was sexually molested by a family member.

When Sherry, with her extensive knowledge of incest, assures me that my extreme feelings are normal, I believe her. When she tells me my father fits a classic picture of one type of incest perpetrator, I believe her. She also says I may continue to experience the return of memories and encourages me to let them come.

Drawing on the experiences of other incest survivors, she helps me deal with what molestation means in my life today. She gives me statistics: One out of three or four women has been molested by the time she is 18, one out of six by a family member. Not once does she question whether my memories are real.

"Have you ever been suicidal?" she asks.

"No."

"Addicted to drugs or alcohol, or do them now?"

"No."

"Ever had a breakdown or been in a mental institution?"

"No." I sit stiffly on the edge of the couch and begin to share what I remember. Sherry explains that dissociating is a common, sane response to incest; amnesia, an effective means of enduring what's unendurable. The child often has no place to turn. No one to tell. No support.

"You're fortunate that you're creative. Your imagination helped you escape," says Sherry.

"I think you're right," I say.

"Some children have psychotic breaks that result in schizophrenia or multiple personalities. They can't handle the incest any other way," says Sherry. "It's a testament to your survival ability that you didn't—or that you didn't show other extreme reactions. Many survivors turn to suicide, drugs, and alcohol. Others end up in abusive relationships or have eating disorders. I know the abuse had a major effect on you, but it could have been worse."

For the first time since remembering, I truly believe that maybe the amnesia was the best I could do. I relax and lean back on the couch.

"Women have amnesia about incest until they feel safe enough to handle what they couldn't as children," she explains.

"In my case, I think being in a good relationship gave me security," I say. "Also, the universe flattened me with an illness that stripped my defenses."

"Remembering is painful," she says in a caring tone. "But know that it will help you reclaim your life. Not remembering blocked vitality in you that could have been channeled in more life-affirming ways. In a sense, you learned to repress *yourself*. Sharing the secret gives you back that energy."

I experience a flash of sadness. "All my life, I've been aware that I held myself back in some way I never understood. No matter how many breakthroughs I had, as soon as I'd start moving forward, bam. This big black boot would come down from the sky and squash me like bug. I'd come up against a barrier I couldn't budge and couldn't figure out why. Now I can. But the whole idea of sharing the incest still makes me feel so vulnerable, stigmatized."

"The burden of incest is terrible," Sherry says. "But you're not responsible for what happened. Your father's 100 percent responsible. He was the adult. You were the child. By keeping this secret, you've taken care of him. Now it's time to take care of yourself."

"Rationally, I know you're right, but inside I still feel like something I did or said brought it on—or worse—I deserved it," I say. "One memory in particular upsets me."

I hesitate. Shame overwhelms me. "Sometimes I felt pleasure when he touched me. How could I feel that?" I expect Sherry to be disgusted, to cry out that I had indeed been a heinous child who invited the molestation.

"Many women felt pleasure when they were molested," she answers, without skipping a beat. "Genitals are made that way. You stroke them; they respond with pleasure—sometimes, even when they're touched by a perpetrator. Besides, incest may have been the only time your father gave you affection—inappropriate as it was. Thankfully, you got some small thing that wasn't pure horror. Don't feel guilty."

I pick up one of the stuffed animals next to me, a brown teddy bear, hold it close. "Maybe feeling those sensations, I sent out the signal that it was okay for him to continue," I say, my throat and body constricting.

"I know that you didn't do what I'm about to say," Sherry says. "But I don't care if you walked up to him stark naked and begged him to have intercourse. You were the child. Children often don't fully understand what they're saying. It was still 100 percent his responsibility to do nothing. Except perhaps tell you to put your clothes back on. You had 0 percent responsibility."

A layer of shame lifts. If Sherry doesn't think I'm responsible or crazy, maybe other people won't either. Maybe I can share this, begin to release this burden.

The session ends with Sherry telling me that the first weeks of remembering are the roughest and to call if I need to talk. I schedule another meeting for two days later. She also hands me a list of books on incest and the name of a women's bookstore that stocks them.

I walked into Sherry's office a quivering wreck, doubting my sanity. I walk out realizing that, yes, I'm in pain. What I went through is terrible. Yet for the moment, I feel good about myself. She got me in touch with my own sense of power, with how emotionally healthy I am—in spite of the incest.

Reclaiming the
Three-Year-Old's Voice

By the time I arrive at Philippe's for our second session, I've struggled through several books from Sherry's list and met with her a second time. Every bit of limited energy and concentration I have during the day, every thought and most of my dream time is consumed by incest.

For now, it has superceded illness as the more pressing crisis. Oddly enough, remembering has even given me new hope for healing. *If I survived sexual abuse, one of the worst things a person can survive, I can certainly survive and heal CFS.*

"I'd like to go back into that first time," Philippe says.

I've anticipated this and agree. Once more, as I lie on the healing table, he directs energy and heat to various parts of my body. He presses my abdomen, and I am right back in the terror. Three years old, gasping, clawing for air.

Terror and anguish rip the guts out of me like one swift scoop of a sharp knife. Who is that whimpering child, totally out of control with panic? Can't be me. Isn't me, won't be me. Won't.

Is me. Simpering, tiny sounds, throat tight, heat flushing my face and chest, buttocks tight, arms weak. Like in a dream, I am unable to lift my arms, unable to run, wanting to run, to escape, to run and never stop.

But I don't run. I stay. And the images come.

It's afternoon, and my mother is gone. My father, his voice tense, calls me into the sea of green that is our living room. He sits in his green armchair. A green area rug with its swirling leaf patterns, green walls, and a green couch encircle him. I am aware of the sun shining outside the two small living room windows, but its rays never stretch into our always dark apartment.

My father's brown hair recedes slightly at the temples. It is combed straight back in a style that accentuates his strong angular features, high cheekbones, and long aquiline nose—slightly crooked from his days as a boxer. He wears tan-colored tailored pants and a brown belt—but no shirt. He often walks around the house this way—or completely naked. "It's more comfortable and natural," he says, proud of the muscular, broad-chested athlete's body that at the age of 37, he works hard to continue to build and maintain.

Panicky, wondering what I've done, I think I'm going to be beaten. I look to see if I've left a toy on the floor. Without a word, I stand rigid before my father. My dress floats up and off over my shoulders and head. Down come my underpants. Already holding my breath, I go numb as I've learned to do, so that I don't cry and get beaten harder.

He takes me—now wearing only my shoes and socks—onto his lap. He tells me I am a bad girl, and he is going to teach me a lesson. All girls are bad. My mother is too. There's only one thing we're good for, and he will show me what that is now. He takes me over his knee.

I wait for the strike of the belt or his hand. Instead I receive a shock, a new kind of pain, one I don't comprehend. His hand glides over my buttocks, and his finger reaches inside me. I cry out. He tells me to shut up or I'll be sorrier. So I hold my breath until my lungs feel like they'll burst. I mustn't cry. I mustn't. Maybe he'll stop.

He turns me over and looks at my three-year-old face. "You're a slut," he says. "All girls are sluts." I'm confused, not knowing what this word means. He laughs and kisses me on my face. "Why don't you kiss me back?" he asks. "Don't you love your papa? Come closer."

His muscular body feels tense, hard. "Don't pull away," he insists. I squirm, and he slaps my face. He carries me into the bedroom and tells me to lie face down on my parents' bed. The textured-off white bedcover feels bumpy against my face and body. I close my eyes.

"Don't move," he says threateningly. "Don't turn around. Your father is just teaching you."

Behind me, I hear him unhook his belt, unzip his zipper. He gets on the bed, his hands all over me, all over my girl parts, swallowing me up. I don't understand. His fingers reach into me more boldly now, reach in as if they are trying to grab hold of my soul, snatch the core of my being.

Pain sears through me. Face frozen. Body rigid. Fear creeping into the memory of every cell. Imprinted. Implanted. Lost. Lost. I am lost, lost.

Can't speak. Can't think. Can't make sense of what's happening, of certain words. Can't breathe. I know I'll die. He'll kill me if I speak. Die. I want to die, to kill, to scream, but it's like in the dreams. I can't get the scream out. I can't move. Everything is in slow motion. Fingers groping me. Out of my control.

Losing my grip. Floating off. Out. Losing my mind. Gone. Can't stay. Gone. Gone. Will I ever? Consumed. Is there any part that's left? Or is this it? Alone. Alone. Lost and alone.

I leave my body. I am above the bed in a corner of the room, looking down on this huge man about to crush a child underneath him. I see the crib I still sleep in, my parents' blond wood dressing table, the closet door.

Then, I am out of the room completely. I've gone to what seems like another land altogether. There are beings with smiling faces and tremendous light. They wear long robes. I want to go with them.

But I don't. I can't leave the body alone in that room.

So I come back. My face on the bed. I am drowning. My body crushed under the weight of this man, under the weight of his words. He tells me I deserve this. I'm a stupid girl, and he can do anything he wants, because he is my father. Something hard rubs on my back. I feel warm, sticky liquid. "See what you did to me, bad girl," he says.

I don't know what's happened. Is he bleeding? Did he pee on me? He carries me into the bathroom and washes us clean. "Stay quiet, bad girl," he says. "If you even think of telling your mother, I'll know. I will kill you both. Understand. Don't think I won't. Nobody would care if two stupid girls were dead."

With that, he leaves me. Alone. I am three years old and have just been raped by my father, without even knowing what that is. Naked, I lie down on the cold green tile floor and curl up into a ball.

This is only the beginning.

Philippe speaks to that wounded child of me. As we did in the previous week's session, he empowers her by leading me through steps to give her a voice. "You're bad, not me," I scream at my father over and over again. "Get away from me. Get off of me now."

"Push hard against my hands, and tell me that," Philippe says. "Push as hard as you can."

And I do push, my strength pitted up against Philippe's. He leans over me on the healing table, and I imagine shoving my father off and away in the present, as I could not in the past. I scream, repeat, "Get off of me. Get off of me, you evil man. Get away. I'll never let you hurt me again."

Rage comes, then tears. Slowly, these are replaced by a sense of relief, gratitude: To finally know. To finally see.

And this is what I find scattered in the dust of the powerlessness that I thought would overwhelm me if I ever dove in headfirst.

It didn't.

I am not overwhelmed.

In real life, back in my West Hollywood apartment, though, I cannot push my father away as easily as I do that afternoon with Philippe. He is in my face daily.

As I lie resting on the burnt orange couch in our living room, looking out sliding glass doors onto the ferns, flowers, and vines on our patio, he lies beside me. As I process the incest on the navy-blue futon in the second bedroom, he sits beside me. As I shower, and the water floods me with memories, he watches. As I make the short drive from my West Hollywood apartment to my doctor's appointment, he accompanies me. As Jonah and I eat at an open air market, and I wonder if the handsome man at the next table is molesting his young daughters, my father eats with us.

He invades my dreams, too. In one, I am in the dark being raped, suffocated by the weight of a figure with indiscernible features. Next, I am an adult. My father, looking like he did when he molested me, laughs as he grabs at my breasts and crotch. He takes a firm hold of me and climbs on top of me. "Not again," I scream. I try in vain to push him away, twist out of his arms. "No. No. No..." I wake up panicky, sobbing, choking.

Worst of all, in my waking life, my father stares back at me in the mirror every single day. His own face merges with my own. By look, I am my father's daughter. We have the same angular features and high cheekbones, the same long nose. Mine even has a slight bump on it, like his, from where the neighbor boy hit it accidentally with a baseball bat.

I may not be able to change my face. I may not be able to stop thinking about him. But I do decide that, at least, I want all other reminders of this man gone. I pile all the photographs of him I can find on our dining room table and tear them up one by one. I destroy every gift he and his present wife, Margo, brought me from their world travels. A garnet necklace from India. A string of coral beads from Mexico. A mug from Israel. A stuffed Koala bear from Australia. All physical remnants of our life together fit into one paper grocery bag. I personally deposit it into the basement dumpster.

My anger continues to erupt. I imagine murdering my father—a process I learned in Gestalt therapy. While I would never commit this act in real life, I give myself permission to repeat it again and again in my mind's eye.

In this realm, I take a sharp surgeon's knife and mutilate my father's body. A once-acclaimed swimmer and boxer in Latvia, the country he grew up in, he still competes in Masters swimming tournaments in the United States. His body remains his pride and joy, the source of his esteem and power in the world. Piece by piece, chunk by chunk, I dismember it. An arm here, a foot there. Here a penis, there a testicle. All appendages. Chop them up into little bits. But throughout, I keep him alive and suffering, conscious.

I bring in his beloved wife, Margo, murder her slowly and painfully. I don't have anything against her. This is simply the worst thing I can think of to do to him.

As he loses consciousness, I tell him I will dump his body parts on the largest, stinkiest garbage dump in the world—Staten Island. Here, mountains of reeking garbage stretch for miles. This holy ground of the rats will be his final resting place. Who knows what beastie will nibble away at his remains?

My father is a clean freak—a reaction, he told me, to the poverty and filthy house of his youth. He can't stand any dust or marks, washes a dish as soon as he finishes eating, and won't even cook with spices because he doesn't want lingering odors. I imagine his alarm, his terror. I laugh in his face as he dies.

Like an obsessive-compulsive washing her hands over and over again to extricate all germs, I expand, fill in the details of torture over and over, constantly refining. An extra body bit here. A stab there. Using my limited energy, I act it out in the safety of my meditation space. I punch at pillows, kick at the futon. With each action, I let out whatever screams, words, and primal grunts want to emerge. No thoughts of the Divine or forgiveness here.

Speaking the image out loud, I own it even more. I offer it up for witnessing to Jonah, to Sherry, to Philippe. And slowly, slowly, the rage releases and transforms.

Ultimately, I will come to realize what the best revenge I could ever level against my father is. That is for me to live my life as loudly and flawed-humanly fully as possible, to be it all, in truth and in love.

Soon afterward, for the first time in six months, I experience more energy. I celebrate by going to brunch with Jonah in Venice Beach. We walk three blocks and back on the boardwalk and sit on the beach for an hour. Two weeks earlier, I couldn't do either. I'm still dealing with full blown CFS. Some days and weeks remain better or worse. But, my "high" energy point has definitely been upped a notch.

This feeds my belief that CFS and the incest are interconnected. Perhaps I became susceptible to illness because of the abuse and the stress it engendered. I'm optimistic that as I reclaim the energy no longer used to suppress incest memories, I'll experience both emotional and physical healing.

This is the carrot I hold up for myself, the Powerball lottery I want to win. It's a possibility my MD, Jim, Philippe, and Sherry all support.

In fact, Jim, a staunch believer in the mind-body-spirit connection, has actually witnessed chronic and supposedly terminally ill patients get well after they get to the psychological roots of traumas. "Healing a serious illness isn't just about working on the body," he says. "It's also about healing your mind and spirit, awakening to a deeper sense of who you are."

Research in psychoneuroimmunology supports this, he explains. It has repeatedly found that significant numbers of adults with severe illness were abused or otherwise traumatized as children. The stress of the trauma, the energy it blocks as repressed emotions and memories, weakens the immune system, making the body susceptible to dis-ease.

"Physicists have already revealed that everything, including a human being, is made up of energy," he says. "So, it makes sense that if you discover and release the source of blocked energy, as you're doing, you can restore your health."

Unresolved abuse issues may not be the only factor contributing to illnesses like CFS. The reading I've done on the mind-body connection also points to other dynamics—life stress, genetics, and environment. On the spiritual side, there's karma and the "I don't know"—the Great Mystery factor.

My goal continues to be to work with whatever I can to help my own healing. At present, that means focusing my attention on the sexual abuse. As this frees energy, the scale now weighted toward illness will, with any luck, tip toward complete recovery.

Thinking this way empowers me. I can work with Jim, Philippe, and Sherry. I can take the herbs and nutritional supplements Jim suggests. And, working daily on the mind-body-spirit connection, I can more actively participate in my own healing.

I spend time each morning sitting or lying on the futon in my office, shades drawn, meditating, asking for support through prayer and listening for intuitive guidance. Using Gestalt therapy techniques and voice dialogue, I converse with different aspects of myself—the wounded child, the critic, the sick one, the inner healer. I process feelings and analyze dreams. Lacking the concentration to write, I speak messages I hear and breakthroughs into a tape recorder. My voice still sounds so monotone from the illness I barely recognize it.

One morning, as I sit silently, meditating in my healing space, these words come—a spontaneous gift of wisdom from an inner teacher, who identifies herself as my "higher self." I hear her words spoken softly inside my head and repeat them into the tape recorder. Henceforth, she will regularly provide perspective and insight: *Honor the groping,* she says that day. *Ride the wave of un-knowing and not knowing. Trust this process.*

What you are experiencing is a dark night of the soul that will eventually lead to an alchemical rebirth. Before you ever came into a body, you chose to have these experiences, not as punishment, but for the learning and soul evolution they would provide. In time, going through and healing the challenges will help you serve as a catalyst of healing for others as well. The lessons and teachings will become clear.

In truth, if the abuse had been too much for you to handle, you would have been removed from the circumstances. You would have died.

Present even now within the limited physical capabilities of your body and the raw wounds of abuse exists a place that is whole. This place has never been damaged, never been touched, and never can be—not by your father, not by any past or present challenge.

You are a divine being. We are all divine beings. As such, you are already healed physically and emotionally, already in a state of divine grace. You have all the resources you need right now to co-create a healing with the Divine, which exists in you and in every being.

These words transport me out of the grip of the incest and illness, out of my darkened room, into a more spacious place. My personal story gives way to a glimpse at a more expanded perspective. I embrace the solace and the hope that this outlook—and my improved physical energy—provide. Eventually, though, as my trials continue, the message slips away into the forgotten recesses of distant memory.

Breaking Patterns and
Speaking Secrets

"Where was your mother during all this?" Sherry asks in one of our sessions.

"Honestly, I've been so focused on my father, I haven't thought much about her in relation to the incest," I say, pausing to gather two stuffed bears and a lamb around me. My resistance to dealing with my mother rises. But I take a deep breath, pull the animals close to my solar plexus, and continue. "She definitely witnessed the physical and emotional abuse. She would try to talk my father out of beating me. He probably would have killed me if she hadn't been around. But she didn't stop it."

"So she didn't condone what was going on?" asks Sherry.

"No, definitely not—nor did she hit me," I respond. "In fact, even though she herself admits she made mistakes in raising me, she was also the only parent who gave me love. She was the one who cared for me and played with me. She took me to dance classes and came to my recitals. She hugged me a lot. But I didn't trust her love. I'd ask myself, *How could she care and still allow the abuse?* I've already worked a lot on my feelings about this in therapy over the years."

"Do you think she knew about the incest?" Sherry asks.

I think for a moment. "My initial hit is, no. I don't know if she saw any signs."

"She may have seen something and ignored it—not even intentionally," says Sherry. "In those days, parents didn't know how to look for indications. Also, for most women, the husband was the sole financial support. To see incest would mean breaking up the family and losing that support. That helped mothers deny anything they might have seen or suspected."

I feel an unsettling mix of both anger and compassion for my mother and squeeze the stuffed animals even more tightly to me—as if I'm holding both them and myself. One possible "sign" that my mother didn't recognize flashes into my mind. "I do remember one thing," I say. "When I was three, I stopped eating. Out of nowhere. Even with coaxing, I'd only eat the smallest portion of food. The doctor couldn't find anything physically wrong, so he gave me vitamins. He never explored possible emotional causes. After quite a while, I just started eating again. I probably stopped when the incest began."

"That sounds right," Sherry says. "A young child stopping eating is a pretty strong signal." She pauses. "Tell me about your parents. What was their relationship like?"

I relate that they met as refugees in a displaced person's camp in Bavaria after World War II. Both had escaped from Latvia, their homeland, as the Russian Front advanced and occupied it. This wasn't the first occupation of Latvia. The country had been oppressed for 700 years by Russia, Germany, and other countries, had tasted freedom only between WWI and WWII.

My mother married Voldemars, my father, soon after graduating from high school at the camp, where they both had lived for several years. She was 19, had been raised in rural Latvia. Her parents, successful farmers, had escaped during the war as well. My father was 31, city-bred, from a poor, uneducated family. He'd dropped out of school at 13 to work after his father died of cirrhosis, and had eventually become a well-known athlete in his small homeland. He'd come to the camp alone. His mother, his only remaining family, had been hit by a bus, killed when he was 18.

My parents immigrated to the United States in 1949 and settled in Cleveland, Ohio. There, my father found a job as a blacksmith in a steel mill.

"Did your father abuse your mother, too?" Sherry asks.

"I don't remember him hitting her," I answer. "But he yelled at her all the time. And he put her down. He'd tell her she was ugly. And nothing she did was ever good enough. Cooking. Cleaning. He got jealous when she gave me attention. And it wasn't only verbal. Sometimes, he wouldn't talk to us for days, just fume. They finally separated when I was 17."

"Is it possible either of your parents was sexually abused?" Sherry asks. "Often, incest survivors come from parents who were abused. The cycle can repeat for generations until a survivor finally deals with the problem and breaks the pattern."

"It's possible," I tell her. "My father's father was an abusive alcoholic. He beat and verbally abused my father and his own wife, who was chronically ill with crippling arthritis. Maybe he sexually abused my father, too. And my mother? She definitely wasn't aware of any sexual or physical abuse by her father. But she went to boarding school for two years when she was 13 and 14. At the refugee camps, her family shared close, open quarters with hundreds of strangers. Maybe she was molested. But neither she nor my father is conscious of sexual abuse. If it happened, they blocked it out."

"It does sound like a possibility," Sherry says. "In any case, they've both experienced considerable trauma and upheaval."

"Yes, they have," I say. "But one thing I know. That cycle of abuse stops with me. I'm healing this."

"You're breaking the family pattern—and the silence," says Sherry. "That's already healing."

"It is. And I'm feeling strong enough to take this one step further. I'm going to start telling other people about the abuse," I say. "Beginning with my friends."

"That's a good idea," Sherry answers. "It's so healing to stop carrying the secret alone. Just do it on your own terms. Tell as much or as little as you want when you want. You've nothing to be ashamed about."

I systematically start telling my friends. As I speak the words I've held and measured for so long, they flood out in torrents. I pace my life so that the energy I have can go into informing friends about it. I relate my recaptured history face to face, one friend or one couple at a time, most often while we go out to eat together. Jonah often accompanies me. For out-of-town friends, I speak the words into a tape recorder—since the illness still limits my letter writing ability—and then I mail them the tapes.

The more I speak the words, the more I want to, must speak them. I become a woman obsessed with telling. And not only friends. I am tempted to grab strangers off the street and tell, to sit at bus stops and wait for unsuspecting people coming to catch the bus to tell. I want to tell every grocery or retail clerk or telemarketer who asks me, "How are you today?" But I don't. I stick to telling my friends. Bit by bit, I feel the poison, which has choked me for a lifetime, begin to lose its grip.

One day during a meditation, an experience comes that contrasts sharply to this process of telling. I sense a wordless, voiceless gagging. A picture emerges in my mind of a shapeless being with a black hole where the face and mouth and features should be. I feel its constrictions in my own throat.

It seems to be trying to speak, but I can't make out any words or sounds. I wonder if it's another incest memory trying to emerge. I coax it to speak louder, imagine it and me in a completely safe, protected space. Still, I hear no response. I only sense choking and a bottomless sadness, an intimation of a crushing load. Over the next days, the image and sensations come time and again. But I can never see the being's true form or hear its voice in the blackness.

I tell Philippe about it in our next session. Instead of working on the healing table, he suggests we sit and talk in the living room. I choose a peach-colored couch; Philippe, a plush mauve armchair. Together, we invite the faceless one to come into the light and sit next to me.

Slowly a child's face appears in my mind's eye. Without any visible body. The first sound of her voice emerges in my head, too. Primal, guttural sobs. Gradually, I see. She is me at seven.

"What does she want to say? Why is she crying?" Philippe asks.

He suggests I move to the spot where I've imagined the child sitting and talk out loud as if I'm her, allowing her answers to come through my voice. Finally, she speaks. She tells us a memory of being in the shower with my father, of him forcing her head down, of feeling like she was drowning, of the incest escalating at that point to include fellatio.

At seven, the child comprehends more fully what's happening to her. It's as if her father putting his penis in her mouth also corks up her voice, shuts down even more of her ability to express herself freely. She shares the deepening despair and shame. She feels so alone. She doesn't think she can go on. She wants to die. Abruptly, she stops talking, refuses to continue.

"What's wrong?" Philippe asks. "You don't have to censor yourself. You're safe here. You made it. You grew up to be an adult. You can say anything you want; we'll accept you. Tell her that, too, Vita."

I move back to my part of the couch and speak as the adult me again.

"Little one, I'm here for you now—always, no matter what. I'll never leave you alone," I say, breathing deeply to open my heart to her anguish. "I want to listen to anything you tell me. I promise I won't let your father or anyone ever hurt you again."

Once more, I move into her spot and wait for her answer.

"I had a...secret place," she says, haltingly. "A place I went during the incest. I left my body and traveled there when my father abused me. I never told anyone about it, not even you. It was my only safe place. The place where no one—not he, not even my mother—could find me. I've been afraid to tell, because then it might not be safe anymore. I might not be able to get back there, or you might think I'm crazy."

"I'd really like to know about this place," I say, surprised at her response. I had expected her to relate still another difficult memory.

"It was a real place with bright green grass and trees," she says. "Everything was soft and gentle. Loving people, who wore long, white robes lived there. They held me and played with me. They told me I could come to them when I needed to get away from my father."

I remember I'd flashed on an image of these beings when I first re-experienced leaving my body in the earlier session when I had returned to the initial molestation. As the seven-year-old tells me about them and her secret place, I sense a lightness, a brightness, a joy—the first I've felt since remembering the abuse, and certainly nothing I expected to feel today after recalling the fellatio. "Thank you. Thank you for telling me and for trusting Philippe. I can sense this place," I say. "I'm so grateful you had somewhere to go." She releases a big sigh. It reverberates deep inside me.

Once again in my seat, in my mind's eye, I see her, full-bodied now. Philippe suggests I gather her to me. She comes willingly into my arms. I hold her and rock her back and forth for a long time.

⌒

For some days following the session with Philippe, the seven-year-old comes forth in the quiet times I set aside for processing the abuse, to fill in the memories of the shower incidents.

"You have a wild imagination," my father often says to me when I am growing up. This is not a compliment. While he speaks the words, his ruggedly handsome face careens out of control, reddening and contorting, ready to explode like the white puss-impacted tip of a boil. Having any type of imagination, particularly a wild one, is a curse, the worst curse possible, he infers. At the very least, it needs immediate containment, and as soon as possible, annihilation and eradication.

Now, I don't remember what specifically I did or said the first time he reared up so against that wild imagination of mine.

I was, in fact, an imaginative child, who loved to create plays and perform all the parts, to paint, to sing, to dance—and secretly to write.

I do, however, remember how he continues to use it against me when he sexually abuses me. In fact, one variation on his threat to kill me if I tell is, "If you tell anyone, I'll say you're crazy. That wild imagination of yours is making you say these things. No one will believe you, not even your mother. They'll lock you up."

Sometimes, he waggles that wild imagination of mine in my face during the incestuous act itself. He plays a sick game, gaslights me by pretending that what is happening isn't really happening.

When I am seven—the second age that has turned up now as particularly significant in terms of remembering the incest, my family and I have already moved from our apartment to a house in a Cleveland suburb. My mother has taken a full-time job. That means that most days, I am alone with my father for two or three hours before she comes home. He returns from working his seven-to-three shift at the steel mill, wearing a steel-gray wool coat and a gray hat. His sullen face and hands are gray, too, from the griminess of his job. He carries his soiled work clothes for the day in a bag.

First thing, he takes a shower in the personal shower stall he built for himself next to the bathtub. Its light golden tiles match those around the bathtub and contrast with the aqua color of the tub and bathroom walls. The floor is covered with aqua and golden squares of linoleum. Often, he makes me take a shower with him. He brings my bath toys into the stall with us—a rubber duck that floats and a pail that, in the tub, I like to fill with water and pour over my head. But before playing, he says, we have to get clean. Under the guise of "washing me, because I am so very dirty," he molests me.

He makes me lather him methodically with soap, too—his firm, muscular torso, penis, testicles, buttocks. "Still dirty," he says. "More. Harder. You didn't get it all."

It is only my imagination that anything is wrong with this,

he says, only my wild imagination that anything unseemly is happening. "Don't pull away," he says. "What's the matter?" After the washing, he faces me away from him. As if by my not seeing what is about to happen, it isn't so, but only that wild imagination again. He tells me to play now.

For a while, I hold my duck with one hand and make a figure eight with it under the shower water. I run my other hand over the slick wet surface of the tiles. I imagine myself diving into their golden color. Behind me, my father stiffens and moans slightly as he shoots a warm, sticky substance onto my back. The shower water quickly washes away all evidence of his misdeed down my legs into the drain. In remembering these showers, they are as much a brainwashing as they are molestation, confusing my images of what is right and wrong, of what happened and what didn't.

One day, instead of turning me away from him, he faces me toward him. That's when the incest escalates. That's when he forces my head down, forces me to take him into my mouth. I remember water streaming down my hair and face. I choke on steamy liquid, on the fullness of him, on my growing awareness of the unnaturalness of this act. Face to face with my father's naked body, mouth stuffed with penis, I have no place to look away, to distance myself from the horror of this new level of wounding.

When I tell my father I don't want to take a shower with him, that I don't like showers, he simply blames it on that wild one again. "It's only your wild imagination," he says. "Showers are fun. We get to play games together. Here, let's bring in your bath toys." And the showers continue.

That winter of my seventh year, I get a flu that keeps me out of school with a raging fever for three weeks. When the doctor makes a house call to give me a penicillin shot, I scream and resist. My parents hold me down on my bed until he finishes. Later, after using the medicinal gargle he prescribes, I vomit again and again.

I also become extremely nearsighted, no longer able to read the numbers on the blackboard at school, and have to wear glasses. "It's all that reading she does," my father says. "It's that imagination of hers. She loves those books, and now they've ruined her eyesight."

And, every evening, before bed, I always take a bath—even through my teenage years. Before remembering the incest, I simply think that I hate taking showers.

Whenever I think about them, my wild imagination seems to run away with itself—like my father warned me. I can't shake a picture I have of almost drowning in the shower as a younger child.

That image is so vivid. Water surges up my nose and fills my throat. My throat tightens. I choke and sputter. My lungs hurt, ready to burst from the pressure, like when somebody holds your head under water for too long. For some reason, I can't lift my head up and out of the endless streams of water to take a deep breath. I think I am going to die in the shower.

I ask my mother if I ever almost drowned in our shower. She looks at me quizzically. "It's just your imagination," she says. But she never does force me to take showers while I am growing up. I take baths until I go to college, where the dorms only have shower stalls.

Years later, when I tell Chris, a friend from college days, about the abuse, she recounts, "I never did understand, until now. When I first came to spend a weekend at your house, you insisted I not take a shower in the shower stall, but only in the bathtub. You made this huge deal about it—about how bad things could happen in there. I thought it was some weird phobia."

Wild imagination, indeed. My family may tell me that I'll get hurt beyond repair if I get involved with it—and the images it shows me do hurt sometimes. But the other side of that wild one is this freedom and creativity that make me feel more alive than anything else. So I hold onto its wildness, hide it from my parents and everyone else, have a secret rendezvous with it, feel its electric heat. I want it, yearn for it.

Sometimes, that wild one and I take flight together. We fly high, high up into the sky, up to the source, its home, its heat, the sun. We fly up through rainbow colors to white light like nothing I've ever seen. We fly closer and closer, my wild spirit unleashed. Outside all bounds of safety, my senses finely tuned, images flood me.

But each time we fly, at some point, the heat begins to burn and scald my skin. What before felt warm, nourishing, expansive gives way to darker, more foreboding, suffocating images—hints of something locked away, something that is better kept that way, something too horrible to unleash.

While growing up, I can't have that wild one in my life completely without unlocking that door. Yet what lies beyond seems overwhelming. I am too afraid to move forward with my passionately expressive one. So I turn back. I tumble, tumble back to earth, wings singed, burned down to bone, two unusable little stumps. I hit the ground hard, emerging back into a world of gray sameness. It is the same color as the coat and hat my father wore to work. It is the same color as the gray zone of CFS.

I don't know I will have to open that door and let those shadowy images materialize fully to reach the radiance beyond, bask in the shining light that doesn't damage. This pure white blaze sears away only that which stands between me and my authenticity.

Funny thing, how back then, in childhood, much of what is referred to by my father as my wildest imagination is not imagination at all, but *truth*. Glimpses of what really happened. It is those flashes of vision that terrify me as a child and young adult. They teach me that maybe my father is right. Perhaps I do need to curb that wild one.

After all, that wild imagination seemingly forces me back then to feel what I cannot allow myself to feel, comprehend what is incomprehensible, taste what gags me, hear what deep in my belly makes me retch, and smell that which disgusts me. Better to deny it, disclaim it, tuck it away. Better to block it out than to recognize that the man I am supposed to trust above all others to protect and love me is a crazy, abusive pedophile.

But I never totally let go of that beloved imagination, that creativity, which is my very lifeblood. I simply learn to turn my life force down to quarter volume. Just enough to stay alive. Just enough to help me survive those early years without going crazy or killing myself. Just enough to face what follows in adulthood as well. But not enough to be vibrantly alive.

Even now, the volume controller, the voice that emerged to protect me then and has continued to protect me even when I haven't needed that kind of protection anymore, rears up again and whispers in my ear. "Stop what you're doing. You're crazy. Shut up. Don't speak. Don't tell any of it. You'll die. If they don't kill you, I will." When I first became aware of this voice and its function, I tried to squelch it, like I had been squelched.

But now, I embrace it, recognize it as my ego insinuating itself into my consciousness again. I send it love. I remind it of its new job title, Passion Truth Promoter, and give it a second one—Healthy Balancer. I explain that our life depends on ardent expression now, on truth speaking, on accessing all volumes. It needs to ride the winds on the broad back of that wild imagination—through forests and mountains, up to the heavens and down into the deepest infernos.

I listen to this voice when it speaks. Sometimes it even tricks me into being afraid or feeling overwhelmed again. It knocks me down like the school bully, and I shrink into myself for a time. But I always rise again. I am stronger than it now, stronger on levels I don't even know. I am stronger than anything that happened to me, and I tell all of it.

———

This is what I remember before I remembered the incest, the childhood I thought I lived. When I start first grade, we move from a small apartment into a yellow brick, ranch-style house with two picture windows. My father built that house with his own hands, brick by brick, after work and on weekends. He wanted big picture windows, he said, so that sunlight would flood the place. He could see space around him. And I, his child, wouldn't grow up in cramped poverty like he had.

This three-bedroom house in the suburbs of Cleveland is supposed to make everything better. It signifies that my father finally achieved something in his adopted land. Other Latvian émigrés, who still lived in apartments or with their parents, will now respect him. His job in the steel mill, which feels stultifying, will become more tolerable. He and my mother will once more melt into the love that had bonded them. We will be a real family.

But the night before we move in, my mother sees a big gray rat in front of the sandstone fireplace in our new living room. It's the same fireplace that we'll never use, because my father doesn't want ash and soot to mar its walls. My father chases that rat with a broom, corners it in the fireplace, stuns it. With his bare hands, he breaks its neck.

Afterward, he collapses, hunched over on the floor, his head in his hands, shaking back and forth. "Seeing a rat before you move into the house is bad luck," he moans. "There will be no happiness for the people who live there."

"It's only a superstition," my mother says. "We'll prove it wrong."

"I hope you're right," he says. "But I don't feel good about it."

That night, we do something we never do as a family. My father gathers us in a circle near the fireplace, a picture window on either side of us. He prays for God to remove the curse of the rat and bring us happiness in this house. I pray along, fervently hoping our heartfelt plea will indeed bring a melody to the cacophony that is our family. Still, rat or no rat, in the pit of my stomach, I cannot imagine it.

⌒

The new house sits on a busy, two-lane county highway. The neighboring houses, all unique, built in different time periods by different families, range from an old one-bedroom wood cottage to a 16-room brick home with a pool. Our suburb is the fastest-growing in the Cleveland metropolitan area, surging from 5,000 people when we move in to 19,000 only 10 years later.

I would rather live in one of the new developments on a quiet street, where all the houses are the same, and there are lots of children to play with. By our house, there are only three children, the neighbor's—all older or younger than I am, and we don't get along.

In the new house, though, I do finally have room to breathe, places to play and a room of my own with a door I can close. And I do love those picture windows that bring in the light of the outside world. One window, which spreads two-thirds the expanse of our living room, looks out on the front yard and the highway. We live on a sharp curve on the road, and about once every year, a car will spin out of control and have an accident. We lose many mailboxes. One 16-year-old boy loses his life.

My parents say it's too dangerous for me to play out there. But I can still look out that window. From second grade on, after my mother gets a job, I am a latchkey child and use the window's view to entertain myself. Since none of the houses has a sidewalk, there isn't much foot traffic. But I watch the cars, make up stories about where each driver is going, what their lives are like. It eases the fear and loneliness I sometimes feel. I imagine what my life would be like if I flagged one down to take me along. I envy those people going somewhere other than where I am.

I perform in front of the window, too. The living room with its muted blue walls and shellacked hardwood floor is my stage. I make believe I'm a famous ballerina, an opera singer, or an actress. I dance and sing and turn and move every part of my body full out, exploding in ways I can't when my parents are home. I race around the inside loop of the house from living room to dining room to kitchen to hallway to foyer to living room. After my parents buy a record player, I perform to their albums—Gilbert and Sullivan operettas, Hawaiian music and Henry Mancini—or put the radio on a rock-and-roll station.

I imagine that people driving by can see me through the window. First one, then every passing car stops, magnetized by the sheer magnificence of my performance. The yard fills with people who want to watch. Completely absorbed in my spontaneous show, I remain unaware of their presence. When I finish, I look up, surprised to see the crowd. My audience breaks into applause. I take bow after bow and always perform an encore.

I imagine that one drive-by audience member is a famous movie director—who happens to be passing through my suburb. Awe-struck by my talent, the director rescues me from my father's abusiveness and takes me to Hollywood. I become a star and get the attention and praise I crave.

Years later, when I'm an adult, the therapist I worked with before remembering the incest says that even though my parents shouldn't have left me alone, their neglect ultimately worked to my advantage. The freedom I had to explore my spontaneous impulses and nourish my creative spirit probably saved my life.

~

The other picture window of my childhood home looks out on the natural world of my backyard. Its centerpiece is an oak tree that stands at least 50 feet tall. I yearn to climb it, but can't reach even its lowest branches. I settle for climbing the young maples that line our yard's boundary. From one spot on a certain tree, I can see when my mother walks home from the bus stop.

I watch the wildlife that graces that yard. Chipmunks dart in and out of the rock garden my father built. Squirrels bury acorns. My cocker spaniel chases rabbits, but when she and a pheasant come face to face, both run scared in opposite directions from each other. After cold, gray winters, the arrival of robins heralds the promise of warmth and the new life of spring. I wish I had shoes the color of the cardinals that feed in the grass. One fall, a flock of hundreds of blackbirds heading south congregates on the ground and trees in our yard. It looks like a scene out of Alfred Hitchcock's *The Birds*, where birds start pecking people to death. But I'm not scared of these birds. I feel special somehow, honored they chose our yard for their respite. When noises startle them, they fly up, hover overhead, and return. A sea of birds undulating as they rise up in the sky and back down again. It is a sacred moment.

⌣

Most of the time, however, I am in that backyard, rather than looking at it. We own a full half-acre with a stretch of woods behind it. There I don't have to worry so much about talking too loudly. I run through sprinklers, swing on my swing set, or throw wormy, green apples from our apple tree for my cocker spaniel to chase. I play with my best friend Baiba.

Both Baiba's parents work, too, and our fathers play volleyball together. From the time we are seven years old until junior high, when she dumps me for another best friend, we spend most weekends and summers together at my house or hers.

It is nighttime. Baiba and I are 10 years old and have been put to sleep in my double bed with the beige wood headboard. The bed is part of a matching bedroom set my grandparents bought for me. I picked it out myself. It includes a dresser with a mirror.

The time has come to play one of our favorite games, inspired by a movie we saw where a villain tied a damsel in distress to the train track. A handsome young stranger rescued, then fell in love with her. In our version, one of us first plays the evil villain. The other one plays the victim, the helpless, but beautiful woman, who's been captured and tied up. The evil man does evil things. He kisses her forcibly and hard on her mouth and on her chest. He strips her naked, hurts her. Terrified, the woman in our game struggles, but has no way to escape. If she doesn't agree to marry the villain, he threatens to kill her by tying her to the railroad tracks—like in the movie. She doesn't cooperate. So he ties her to the track.

That's when the gallant young man shows up. Now whoever plays the villain transforms into the hero. He fights off the villain and rescues the woman a second before the train crushes her. They fall in love at first sight. She is damaged, but he heals her. He tenderly puts medicinal salve on every part of her body that hurts. He holds her tenderly. She is so grateful and slowly regains her health. They kiss sweetly. The woman knows her young hero will protect her forever, that no evil man can ever harm her again. They live happily ever after.

Once Baiba and I finish a game, we switch and whoever was the woman first is now the villain.

Both of us always want to play the defenseless woman first. My favorite part is when the hero rescues me. I love it when Baiba's gentle fingers heal the broken places. I love it when her breath comes close, and her lips touch my face. Once, when I think I've given her more time as the woman than she's given me, we argue. From then on, we look at the clock before the game, so that each one of us gets to be the woman an equal length of time.

⌒

In the new house, my father no longer dares smash in walls he built himself. But his abuse of my mother and me continues unabated. And I witness regular reminders of his seemingly indomitable strength.

One evening, when I'm eleven, my parents and I are eating dinner at our yellow Formica kitchen table. It and the countertops match yellow squares on the yellow and blue linoleum floor. The blue squares match the kitchen walls and appliances.

Unexpectedly, my father hands me a carving knife that has a pointy end and a sharp blade. He bends his arm, flexes his formidable bicep, like the body-builders he emulates, so that it bulges. "Go on," he taunts. "Try to jab the knife through my muscle. I'm so strong you can't cut me. You can't even make a scratch." Over and over, he goads. With his other arm, he yanks me up on my feet and makes me hold the knife right up against his muscle. "Go on. Stab it. Hard as you can."

I stand frozen. If I do stab him, I'm not really certain he won't bleed. And if I manage even a tiny scratch, he will lose control. In the heat of his rage, he might even turn the knife on me. At the very least, in his humiliation, he'd beat me. But oh, how I want to try to cut him. For even though I have blocked out the incest at this point, I have not blocked out his emotional and physical abusiveness. So I stand, muscles tense, holding the knife, hatred walling my heart. I want to jab him hard, to give back even a little of the pain he has caused me.

My mother pleads with him to stop. But he yells at her to stay out of it and sneers. "She can't hurt me. She's not strong enough." Holding my arm with a vice grip, he laughs in my face. I am paralyzed, a tiny rabbit with the rage of a tiger locked in her heart. I want to be dead. I want him dead. I want to plunge that knife not into his arm, but into his heart. I want to run from his voice, from my shame and from my own and my mother's powerlessness. I want to run and never stop running. To find someplace, anyplace that's mine, not his, a place that will always be mine. Alone. Inviolate.

Finally, he pushes me away, tells me how pathetic I am, how weak. He yells at me for not trying, for not believing that I can't hurt him. Still, I notice that he doesn't take the knife and jam it into his own arm. In silence, I take his jeers, knowing by this time that choosing not to speak is most often the least painful alternative. And so, my unspoken responses, my withheld screams are locked away along with all the other words and sounds that fester inside, waiting, begging for release.

We finish dinner in taut silence. The only talk is more chiding. "How could a strong man like me have such a scaredy-cat for a daughter?" my father asks. "You're a chicken." Chicken. Funny, how in my teenage years, that becomes his term of endearment for me. It remains so, even when I grow into adulthood. Chicken. Only he usually adds a Latvian ending to it, one that you'd add to the name of a child to connote their dearness. "*Chicken-iņa*," he would call me. "My little *chicken-iņa*." He would say it not sarcastically, but with love and affection, in the tone of a little boy.

Now, as an adult looking back, I realize this scene with the knife takes place before the incest escalates one last time. Soon after that, I will stop it once and for all.

The molestation started when I was three and continued until I was eleven. It usually occurred once or twice a week before my mother came home from work, during the two hours my father and I were alone.

Those days, he returned from his own job acting almost possessed, rigid, robotic. What I remember most are his eyes— dead, hollow, devoid of conscience. They look through me, like the eyes of a pod person from some X-rated version of *Invasion of the Body Snatchers*. These eyes are capable of doing anything to anyone.

Yet somehow I have made it to adulthood in spite of those eyes, in spite of all the abuse. Now I am remembering enough to heal, and, I hope, to move beyond them. Sitting once more on the blue futon in my spare bedroom office, I start to process the sexual abuse as I've done daily since I remembered it six weeks ago.

A memory drifts in. It's of the first time I made love with my boyfriend. I was a freshman in college, and we'd been dating for three years. He was my first love, and we were both seemingly virgins. The act was tender and awkwardly passionate as such first lovemaking acts often are. Yet when we finished, I felt disconcerted. I knew that virgins bled when their hymen broke and wondered why I didn't. At the time, my boyfriend didn't comment, and I was too caught up in simultaneous feelings of excitement and melancholy to pursue my questioning. *Maybe I broke my hymen with a tampon and didn't notice because I was having my period anyway*, I rationalized.

But now, in my office, a new image flashes into my adult mind and replaces this college-age memory. It's of an earlier time in my life. I'm eleven years old. A budding adolescent, I'm lying face up naked. My father is on top of me moving up and down.

"Not this, too," I, the adult, say out loud to the empty room, to God, to myself. I say it to remind myself that I exist in this moment and begin to sob, shaking my head back and forth. "No," I insist to the air. "No, no, no." Yet this memory too oozes in like sticky warm honey flowing from a piece of honeycomb torn from its hive. It stings like bees indiscriminately attacking the desecrator of their home, their sacred center.

"No," I repeat more vehemently as I think, *How does a person say yes to a life full of images like these?* Then, for no rational or irrational reason, I stop shaking my head, I stop sobbing and do just that. "Yes," I say. "I want all of it. Now."

These are the memories that return of what happened to me at age eleven. Intercourse. I first learn about it in sixth grade when I am eleven—one special class for "girls only" and another for the boys. This is what husbands do with their wives in order to conceive a child, our teacher tells us. I experience an uncomfortable mix of excitement, horror, and curiosity at openly learning about this secret act that results in something called procreation. This is an act so forbidden that our parents even have to sign a note before we are allowed to participate in the class.

I had already learned something about intercourse the summer before sixth grade from my best friend Baiba's neighborhood playmates. One moonless night, we were playing hide and seek in the yard next door to hers, lurking under bushes and behind blackened trees. As we all came screaming out from our hiding places, "In free, in free," we gathered into a circle, and one of the boys started talking about it. "It's called fucking, too, and it isn't only about making babies," he said. "Kissing is part of it. Some people do it just to have fun."

"Fun?" Baiba and I said simultaneously, broke out into giggles. "Ee-yooo. That's awful. How can anyone do *that* for fun?" Baiba said to the boy, several children giggling now. "I don't believe you." "I don't believe you either," the others and I chimed in.

"Your parents do it. All our parents do it," he insisted. "I bet they all do it for fun. I bet we'll all do it, too."

"No way," the rest of us asserted, giggling uncontrollably, one boy purposely falling down onto the cool nighttime summer grass, rolling back and forth laughing. Soon all of us are on our backs on the lawn, rolling and laughing, rolling and laughing, the grass so soft and tickly and refreshing against our bare arms and legs and faces.

Still, later that night, as Baiba and I lay talking in her bed before we go to sleep, we wondered what it would be like. Did our parents really do it? Would we ever do it, even to have a baby? Would we enjoy it? "Not me," I said. "Not me either," said Baiba. "It sounds disgusting." We drifted off to sleep.

The very next summer, before I enter the seventh grade and turn twelve, I am forced to do what we've giggled about this past year. The thing I know husbands and wives do, not fathers and daughters. Nobody taught us about fathers and daughters.

One day, my father takes me by the arm down into the basement with its gray cement block walls. There, he directs me to lie down on some old newspapers near the washing machine and septic tank—enough to cover a large area of the gray concrete floor. As he comes to me, I prepare as I have repeatedly done for years now to be the body robotic, going through the motions, lying there without being there. Instead, this time, as I leave my body, I am pulled sharply back in by an inexplicable pain. It is my father sticking not his fingers inside me like before, but his penis. And just when I think I can't experience anything worse than I already have and still cope, this is worse. My father's penis shreds my virginity. Blood and sperm mingle on the newspaper beneath me. But I can't cry, mustn't cry, not now, not here.

I hope against hope that this new activity will not be repeated. But it is. Several times more, my father takes me down the wooden steps to the basement. One day, when he once more leads me to the basement stairs, my spirit snaps. I'm in so much pain that my will to live crumbles. It's like the fragile anthill my friends and I once kicked away from the sidewalk cracks and watched while the ants scurried in all directions.

I make a choice to face what I believe is certain physical death. I don't care. I already feel dead. In an instant, I know what I must do. As we come to the top of the stairs, I resist him. The angrier he becomes, the more stubbornly I hold against the doorjambs. I am prepared to die. While trying to pull me down the steps, he loses his balance. To catch himself and stop his fall, he lets go of me.

Grabbing this chance, I turn and run as fast as I can to my bedroom. Like in the recurring dreams I have of fleeing from seen and unseen attackers, I run. Only this time, instead of being caught or experiencing the terror of only being able to move in slow motion, I escape. Before my father gets to me, I slam the door and lock it.

My heart pounding, I stand inside my room facing the door. He bangs the door and twists the knob forcefully back and forth. He threatens and yells. But safe inside I stand without speaking a word. In complete silence, I simply refuse to open the door. In that moment, I choose life again and find the strength to endure, regardless of what happens in the next few seconds.

Instead of breaking down the door and murdering me as I expect, my father finally leaves. From the kitchen, I hear the sounds of him making dinner like he usually does on week-nights. I hear the sounds of the knife clicking against the cutting board. It slices food instead of my throat. I hear him pounding away at meat instead of at my body. I hear the clatter of dishes as they're placed on the table instead of breaking over my head.

For a while, I listen, frozen, like a gazelle standing across the wide, wild river from a lion. I stand waiting for my father to return, not quite yet believing that the lion won't leap over the expanse and consume me in one bite. But after time, just as the gazelle finally puts its head down and begins to graze, I slowly walk over to my place of refuge—my orange-cushioned, cone-shaped chair that sits in the corner of my room next to my beige dresser and mirror. The chair has four wooden legs with gold metal trim at each end. I picked it out myself the year before, when my parents and I decorated my room. I also picked out the gold paint that covers three walls and the gold, green, and silver patterned wallpaper that graces the fourth wall behind the dresser.

As I pass the mirror, I catch a glimpse of my reflection. I look the same to myself. Yet everything has changed. I sit down in my chair and do homework until my mother is supposed to come home. Standing on the bed, looking out the wide rectangular window set high near the ceiling, I watch for her coming from the bus stop. She doesn't want to walk on the new seed my father has planted under the front yard oak trees. Grass refuses to grow here. So, she walks along the edge of the street across the entire expanse of our property until she reaches the driveway.

I get down now and listen. She makes her way up the two steps to the front porch. As she opens the front door, I open mine. I still expect that my father will kill me now, or maybe later while I sleep. But he doesn't. We eat dinner and watch TV together in silence. I wake up the next morning groggy, but as alive as ever.

I don't know it consciously, but I have discovered a new level of power in this silent protest. Without a word, my father knows that we have crossed a line and can never return to what has been. And with this act, the incest finally stops.

The Grand Truth Telling

May 1986

"Are you going to tell your mother and father you remember?" Sherry asks me at one of our sessions. This simple question knocks me like a swift left to the chin. My forehead tenses. My breath comes fast and shallow. Telling my friends and knowing I was molested has been challenging enough. But I've avoided any thoughts of telling my parents, who are still alive and very much in my life.

"My father isn't a stable man," I answer, heart pounding, ears ringing, eyes blinking. "He suffers from nervous breakdowns. I'm afraid he'll go crazy, maybe kill me, like he threatened to do when I was a child."

Dappled sunlight streams in through the window behind me and throws a diffuse leaf-like pattern of light and shadow over the hardwood floor and Sherry's face and clothing. My own shadow stretches long and thin in its midst. Sherry leans toward me, says softly, "I'm not saying you have to tell him now. In fact, I suggest you fill out your own experience first. But consider this. Many abusive fathers are master bullies. Your father threatened you and your mother with death. Yet he didn't even hit your mother, who may actually have been able to retaliate. He hit a defenseless child. Did he ever threaten either of you with a knife or gun?"

"No."

"Tell me about the nervous breakdowns."

I relate that about once a year, my father goes into periods of despair and panic. They literally started the day after my mother and I finally left him—in the fall of my senior year in high school. My father called our new apartment, sounding hysterical. My mother went back to the house to talk. He was so out of control, she had to call a doctor. For the next two days, my father cried uncontrollably, took tranquilizers and sleeping pills, and slept. My mother and I stayed until he stabilized enough to return to work.

In the years since then, the breakdowns had turned into two-week events.

"What happens now?" Sherry asks.

"He goes to bed with the window shades drawn and cries for two weeks straight," I say. "During that time, he takes heavy tranquilizers. The rest of the year, he takes what he calls his 'nerve medicine.' Recently, that's been an antidepressant. I have this theory that the day my mother and I moved out, what had been his explosions turned into *implosions*. He pretty much stopped being abusive with me. And I never witnessed him emotionally batter his present wife, Margo, like he did us."

"Has he ever gone to a hospital or tried suicide during an episode?" Sherry asks.

"No."

"Been in therapy?"

"He doesn't think he needs it."

The events are sometimes triggered when he's overwhelmed by sadness about his childhood, I tell Sherry. I usually hear about them after the fact—we generally talk every six weeks. Often, they follow a major change in routine, like a trip.

Sherry offers her professional opinion. "They aren't breakdowns. A breakdown's more serious. They're probably related to his own trauma. I'm sure he feels insane. But to my mind, he uses them to get attention and control people—even if he does this unconsciously. Remember, the pattern emerged when he didn't have you or your mother to beat up on anymore."

"Besides, his new wife would never put up with abuse," I say. I flash on an insight. "And I certainly do feel manipulated by the threat of the breakdowns. I still don't confront him too harshly. Often, I monitor my behavior around him, making sure I'm not too much for him."

"And every time you do, holding back exacts an emotional and physical toll on you," says Sherry. "Clearly, your father has severe problems. But they're his responsibility. You need to take care of *you*, not him. Which brings me back to what we started to discuss—telling your parents."

"Truthfully, I'm still afraid of him," I say.

"I've listened very carefully, and I don't think you're in danger," Sherry says. "Many incest survivors are terrified of being physically harmed if they confront their perpetrators. But this rarely happens. Are you going to continue to let him bully you?"

"*No*," I say with a resolve that surprises me.

"All your life, you've taken care of your father," Sherry says. "It's time to start being a good parent to yourself. One of the best ways I know of is to confront him."

"I need time," I say, grabbing onto my favorite brown teddy bear from her collection, stroking its head and ears. I focus my attention on the pattern of light and shadow on the floor. It moves back and forth as a breeze blows the tree outside. My own shadow remains still.

"Of course," she says, pulling my attention back. "Trust your own timetable. Some survivors don't confront their perpetrators for years. You don't *have* to tell in order to heal. But in my experience, placing the responsibility back where it belongs can help."

I take a deep sigh, hold the bear closer. The panic that registered early in the session is gone. "I don't want to carry this secret alone anymore," I say.

Sherry nods. "One more thing. Tell for you and you alone. Your father may deny the incest. Most fathers do. Some have blocked it out. They have actually dissociated and don't remember. Others don't want to deal with the possible legal ramifications or the impact on their present relationships. Even if he does admit it, you may both choose to end your relationship."

"At this moment, I can't imagine wanting to see him again," I say.

"Also, your mother may refuse to believe you," Sherry says.

"Really?" I feel a fluttering in my chest. My mother and I may have had our problems. We may still have the abuse issues to work out. But we've healed so much. I love her and don't want to lose her. How could she not believe me?"

"I'm not saying she won't," Sherry says. "It's difficult to understand how any mother wouldn't. But you need to prepare for the worst-case scenarios. Incest is so terrifying, that sometimes, the entire family goes into denial. They reject the survivor rather than the perpetrator. Since your parents are divorced, it's less likely."

"Not to mention that my mother still has nothing to do with my father," I say. As I speak, the need to tell both my parents firmly extends its roots and takes hold. No matter what the response, I'm no longer willing to live this lie. I cannot not tell. I focus closely again on Sherry's words.

"In any case, take this step for yourself, not in the hope that anyone will believe or support you. But you don't need to decide now. Think about it over the next weeks."

"I don't have to," I say without hesitation. "I honestly couldn't live with this knowledge without telling my parents. I couldn't talk to my father and pretend nothing is going on. I may not be quite ready, but I'll know when."

⌒

Clearly, the universe thinks that the time is right sooner than I do. Within days, on May 22nd, the telephone rings. It's my father. I would like the events to have happened in the order I've written them in this memoir—with me remembering everything about the abuse before confronting him. In actuality, my father calls three weeks after my first memory, before I recapture the memories of the intercourse.

I have been anticipating his call. The last time my father and I talked, a few days before I remembered, he mentioned that later in the month, he and Margo were planning to drive up from San Diego, where they'd lived since the mid-1970s, have lunch with us, and then drive back the same day. The point was to visit without tiring me too much.

Jonah answers the phone, which sits on the counter between the kitchen and dining room, motions to me, mouths silently, "It's your father." We already have a plan in place to buy some time. "Vita has laryngitis and can't talk," Jonah tells him. "She'll call you when she gets her voice back." A few feet from Jonah, I stand at attention, chuckling silently, a nervous hysteria rising in me. *Yes, laryngitis*, I think, almost believing I actually have lost my voice. *Isn't it funny that I have laryngitis and can't talk to my father even though I'm here?* I imagine him chuckling to himself, too, unaware of the larger drama. "Oh that Vita," he might say to Margo. "Not only does she get sick, but now she has laryngitis, too. What else can go wrong for that girl?" Jonah tells my father he's about to run out and gets off the phone. Thank God, I didn't answer it myself.

So the event I dread is set in motion. As soon as Jonah hangs up, I know I'm not willing to wait any longer. Strength that until now I've been unaware exists in me clicks in.

Two days. I figure I have two days to get it together for the most important confrontation of my life. It will likely be the last conversation my father and I ever have.

I immediately set up emergency appointments with Sherry and Philippe.

"I've decided to confront my father over the phone rather than in person," I tell Sherry. "I'm feeling too physically vulnerable to do it face to face. I'll feel safer knowing he's a few hours away. I also don't want Margo there. Let him decide whether or not to tell her."

"Trust your own instincts," Sherry says. "You know best what you need."

"I also wanted to ask you something. You mentioned in our last session that just like survivors sometimes get amnesia about molestation, so do fathers," I say. "Do you think that's a possibility with mine?"

"There's a chance, considering how emotionally unstable he is. But most fathers who deny it do remember," says Sherry. "They just refuse to admit it. Whether or not he remembers, though, isn't your concern. Your job is to speak your truth with as much support around you as possible."

We discuss various scenarios of what I might say and what reactions to expect. Sherry suggests that I keep notes in front of me and plan the conversation. "Since this may be the last opportunity you have to speak to your father, make sure you get everything in. Also prepare to stand your ground. He'll probably accuse you of being crazy or lying."

"I'll be ready," I say.

We plan for the interaction with my mother in a similar fashion.

By the end of the session, I feel total confidence in my decision to tell my parents. At the same time, I accept that as much as my life has already changed, opening up this secret will alter it even further—and forever transform my parents' lives as well.

⌒

"Think back to your childhood once more," Philippe says during a session the day before I call my father. Philippe and I have decided that the best way to further prepare me for that conversation is a guided visualization. Its purpose will be to tap into the ability I have to be a good father to myself, to love and parent myself in the way I've always wanted and needed to experience from my earthly father.

"Only in this version of your childhood, watch all the old pictures and wounds of abuse dissolve," Philippe continues. "Imagine for a moment that the incest and other abuse never happened. In their place is an image of the father you always wanted. He can look any way you want, any size, shape, age, hair color. Picture that father holding you as a child in his arms, gently and lovingly, telling you how much he loves you—just as you are. Imagine him playing with you, encouraging you, recognizing your special talents. He takes delight simply in your being his daughter, and he loves you—unconditionally. Imagine him protecting you from harm's way. Know that in his arms, you are safe. And remember, this loving father is always inside you now, always with you."

I float in the vision that Philippe spins, and for the first time, contact a father's unsullied love. Gratefully, I bask in a newfound capacity to father myself in a way my own father never did. After this session, I feel ready to call and end the relationship with my earthly father.

On May 25th, I wait until 7 p.m. I know my father's schedule. By this time, he'll have finished dinner, and he and Margo are getting ready to watch a syndicated rerun of *Hawaii 5-0*, his favorite program. They've viewed each episode multiple times. "We don't relate to the new shows on TV," he explained once. "Too much sex and dirty talk." Whenever I went to visit him as an adult, we watched those repeat *Hawaii 5-0*s together.

I've been resting all day to save my energy for this conversation. I've written down everything I want to say on a notepad, reaching for the greatest impact with the fewest words. My notes are in Latvian, the language I choose for this exchange. After nearly 40 years in the United States and 16 years of being married to an American, my father still speaks with a thick accent and understands his native language better.

I speak Latvian, but don't have a huge vocabulary. I have no idea how to say *incest, sex,* or *intercourse*. These words aren't in the small Latvian-English dictionary I have at home. I opt for phrases in Latvian like "touched sexually," using the Latvian word for touching combined with an Americanized Latvian version of "sexually."

Tu mani aiztiki seksuāli tā kā tēvam nav brīv aiztikt savu meitu. You touched me sexually like no father is allowed to touch his daughter. *Tu darīji seksuālas lietas ar manīm ko tēvam nav brīv darīt ar savu meitu.* You did sexual things with me that a father is not allowed to do with his daughter.

I sit in the bedroom office at my desk. My notes are spread neatly in front of me, along with the same knickknacks that sat there when I called my friend Sonia a few weeks earlier. I since learned that when she confronted her parents about her incest, they denied wrongdoing, told her she was crazy and cut her out of their lives and out of their will.

Even though it's still light outside, with the Venetian blinds closed, the room is dark, lit only by a desk lamp casting a warm golden hue. Jonah sits in a chair next to me to lend support. I take some deep breaths and place the call.

"Hello, Papa?" I say. Papa is what I call my father, what I have always called him—the Latvian version of "dad."

"Hello, kid. Let's not talk now," he says. "I'm running to watch *Hawaii 5-0.* Margo is already in the living room. I wanted to tell you we're coming up next Tuesday if that's okay. We'll be there around noon."

"No, it's not okay. Don't hang up. I have something important to talk about," I say in Latvian.

"Can't it wait until Tuesday?" he says. "I really want to see this episode."

"No. It can't," I say, and I plunge in. "I've remembered something. I remember that from the time I was three and for several years after that, you touched me sexually in places and in ways that a father should never touch a daughter. You did things to me that no father should ever do to his daughter. I feel hurt and angry and so sad that I had to experience something like that from you, my own father."

"*Meitin,*" he replies, using a Latvian term of endearment, which translates as "darling daughter." "What are you saying? But I'm so glad you brought this up. After that argument we had last year, this is what you said we should do, right? Talk about problems. Well, we have to get this thought out of your head. You made it up. It didn't happen."

"This isn't something like that," I say. "It's not a misunderstanding we can resolve by talking. I know this happened. And it's not a thought you can take out of my head. You touched me sexually in ways a father should never touch his daughter."

"*Meitiṇ*, this isn't true," he says, his voice rising and crackling with emotion. "I can't believe it." He calls out loudly away from the phone, "Margo, you wouldn't believe what she is saying." Then, he's back talking to me. "My God. The dream. Last night, I dreamt my pockets were full of gold coins. My mother taught me this dream meant something would bring many tears. Now, here you are accusing me. How can you believe it? I'm so ashamed."

"I believe it because it's true," I say without faltering, concentrating only on the words passing between us.

"I never touched you," he says, his voice increasingly hysterical. "My God. I should never have walked around the house naked for so many years. Your mother told me I shouldn't, but I did anyway. I hated to wear clothes. I walked around naked until you were seven. Once later, we all went nude sunbathing together in the woods. We used to take showers together, too. I'd bring in your little toys, and we'd play. Your mother knew. You're confused. This is your imagination that's made it into something terrible. You always had a wild imagination. How could you say this?"

"I say it because I remember it. You touched me sexually, like husbands and wives do—not once, but many times. And for many years, from the time I was three until I was almost 12."

"I hardly ever touched you at all," he says emphatically. "I hardly ever even *beat* you, let alone this. I only strapped you with a belt and stuck you in the closet afterward three times. And that's only when you really deserved it. I told Margo."

He proceeds to recount those times. Once, when I was two, he boasted to dinner guests that I'd been toilet-trained since I was nine months old. I embarrassed him by wetting my pants. That same year, I forgot to wipe my feet at the door. The last time, I didn't want to sit next to my visiting grandmother at the table.

"I don't agree that I deserved to be beaten or stuck in a closet—*ever*," I say. "And I know you hit me *many* more than three times. Anyway, *that's* not what I'm talking about here. I'm talking about *sexual touching*, not beating."

"What's happened to you? Can't you see, it can't be?" he says frantically. "You know I'm a one-woman man. I've been faithful to Margo. I was faithful to your mother. I wouldn't have cheated on her with my daughter."

I am stunned. *As if it would be appropriate to cheat with me if you were not a "one-woman man,"* I think. But out loud, I say, "Papa, you're not going to convince me. I know this happened. For the rest of my life, I'll have to live knowing you molested me and hit me, when you should have protected me."

"Oh Margo," he calls out, away from the phone. "You won't believe what she's saying."

"And, know that I'm not talking to Margo about this," I say. "Make your own choice about telling her."

"Oh I'll tell her all right," he says, then calls out again, "Margo, I will tell you. My God, does Jonah know?"

"Yes."

"How can you do this to me? How can I ever see you again when you think this? I'd be so ashamed. It makes me sick. And how could I see Jonah? Vita, I'm sorry, but I can't see you any more."

"Well, I can't see you either, Papa," I say. "You keep talking about what *I'm* doing to *you*. How do you think I feel telling you this and remembering it? I'm the one who was harmed and did nothing to deserve it. Me. Not you."

"Goodbye, Vita," my father says, his voice now terse. "I'll see you in Heaven. I won't see you while we're living anymore. God bless you and Jonah."

Click. He hangs up the receiver and disappears. Just like that.

Silence. The entire conversation lasted 20 minutes. Throughout, I felt deeply grounded, yet lifted up as well, lovingly held, as if by the arms of the Divine.

I said everything I had planned to say. I did not rage at him, although I gave myself permission if I needed to. Getting across what happened was more important to me than ranting at him. I could always do that later in therapy.

I turn to Jonah. His face is soft and open. He stands and opens his arms. I rise to meet this familiar place, the warmth and sense of home I experience whenever his body meets mine. Here, I am safe. Here as we breathe slowly and deeply together, I stand suspended between what took place and what is yet to be.

After a while, thoughts race back into my mind. I slowly unwrap myself from Jonah's embrace and look into his eyes. He tells me he meditated throughout the entire conversation, envisioned my father and me surrounded and filled with divine light. That's what I experienced—total support in speaking the most difficult words I ever had to speak.

I relate the conversation, and when I get to the "one-woman man" comment, he cuts in. "He knows. He may deny it to you, but I believe that comment shows that he knows. To even consider you like that is something of an admission."

"I guess," I say, "but ultimately Sherry was right. He denied the molestation, and he ended the relationship. The admission is what's missing. I'm happy with the conversation. But I sure would have loved an admission."

"It's not who your father is," Jonah says. "I'm amazed he stayed on the phone as long as he did and admitted so much. How could he act like it's a normal thing to beat a child and stick her in the closet for *any* reason? I'm really proud of you. You were incredible. You sounded clear and strong throughout."

Afterward, I feel many things. Relief at the release of a long-carried burden. Grief at the loss of a father I'd loved despite his past abuse and dysfunction. The child in me is also heart-poundingly shocked to still be alive to experience any feelings at all. This little one expected me to shatter into thousands of pieces simply from speaking the words of truth to my father, to disappear—as if I—and she—had never existed at all.

Instead, I'm very much alive and present. Safe in my own

apartment with Jonah. Still in the body. Breathing in and breathing out.

Goodbye, Papa. Goodbye.

The next afternoon, I call my mother. In my early therapy days, she and I had already had some rocky conversations about my physically and emotionally abusive childhood and our relationship. Although she didn't want to work on herself psychologically the way I was doing at the time, she had listened and responded respectfully. When I asked, she even made changes in how she related to me. But adding incest to the picture is a whole different matter. I'm aware this might be the last time we ever talk.

For this conversation, I bring the incest into the light of day, moving out of my office into the living room. I sit on our burnt-orange, textured couch, as I often do when my mother and I talk on the phone. I glance behind me at a painting from *The Wizard of Oz*, Jonah's and my favorite movie. It's of the yellow brick road leading to Emerald City, all rich greens and yellows. I remember seeing the movie for the first of many times with my mother in a Cleveland movie theater. I clutched her hand in terror when the Wicked Witch appeared. This painting depicts the scene Dorothy, Toto, the Scarecrow, the Tin Man, and the Cowardly Lion first see when they come out of the woods and step into the light. And just as the Wizard's curtains were pulled open in the movie and he was revealed as a fraud, I pull open the curtains in our living room, about to unmask the fraud of my family's life. I look out the sliding glass doors at the vines and ferns on our sunlit patio. Jonah offers to sit with me again, but I want to be alone for this talk.

I have a few highlighted notes, less structured than the ones for my father, written in English this time. My mother and I still generally speak Latvian to each other—though I've long since put an end to the "speak only Latvian with us" command my parents gave me as a child. When I have something important to say, I switch to English, because I can express myself more fully. My mother speaks English fluently, but will still most often answer in Latvian. Before the call, I pray for divine energy to surround and hold me like it did for the conversation with my father. Once more, I feel shored up by unseen helpers and enveloped in light.

My mother answers on the first ring. As soon as I make sure she's free to discuss something important, I tell her I was sexually abused.

"Why are you telling me this? Why now?"

My stomach grows queasy. But I breathe deeply, call in the light again. "Because it happened to me, Mamma," I say, using the Latvian term for mother or "mom" as I always do. "It happened to us. For years, I kept the molestation a secret—even from myself. Now I remember. And, to heal, I need to tell you. I need you to support me by listening."

So she listens, and the words unspoken for so long now flow. "My God, I didn't know," she says, her voice quiet, yet filled with emotion. "I didn't know. I'm so sorry you had to go through that."

"You believe me?" I ask.

"Yes, I do. He was a crazy man," she says firmly. "I believe you."

I am believed. Immediately and without question, I am believed. I have one parent left, the one I've most trusted and counted on, the one I most love.

In that moment, I take my place among the lucky survivors, fortunate in being believed. I don't have to survive alone, rejected by my entire family, which is already so small.

"I need your support, Mamma," I say.

"Yes, of course," she says. "I'll do whatever you want. But I'd also like to ask you something."

"Okay."

"What did he do?"

Feeling grounded and clear, I take a deep breath and tell her about the fondling.

"Are you sure he wasn't just exploring to see how a little girl is built differently down there than a little boy?" she asks.

"Mamma," I say. "He could explore that on you. If he does it on me, that's incest."

"You're right. I'm having such a hard time," she says. "Forgive me."

"Do you remember Papa taking showers with me when I was little?"

"No. I wouldn't have allowed it," she says. "I didn't want you in the shower, because I was afraid you'd fall on the tiles. I always gave you baths. Besides, even when you were old enough to take a shower, you didn't like them. You insisted on baths."

I tell her about the showers, the fellatio, all of it.

"What you went through was so horrible. I am so sorry," she says. And, in those words, she and I are released of the lie we had lived.

———

Early the next evening I call my mother again, relieved to have a witness to even some of what went on.

"I know you and I have talked before about Papa hitting me," I say. "He says he only hit me three times."

"He must be crazy," she says without hesitation. "He's trying to look good for his wife. He used to hit you a lot. We never knew what would set him off."

As Sherry had suggested, I tell my mother about the therapy and ask her to send some photographs of me from ages three to eleven. I explain they might help me remember more details and experience my feelings more completely. My mother agrees. "Do you want me to come to Los Angeles and see your therapist with you?"

"You would do that?" I ask, touched, but surprised. My mother doesn't analyze herself—with or without a therapist.

"Yes, if it would help," she says. "I might be able to answer some questions for her."

"It might help you deal with some of your feelings, too," I say.

"No, I wouldn't participate," she says. "I wouldn't feel comfortable. I'd come to support you."

I tell her I'm grateful, but turn down her offer. Unless she actively takes part, her coming to therapy doesn't feel right. I can probably get any information I need from phone conversations. More importantly, to heal, I need to express any charged emotions—as they come up. I'd feel inhibited with her around.

"One more thing," I say. "Do you think Papa's still dangerous?"

"He might very well be," she answers. "I wouldn't be surprised if this set him off."

As a precaution, I ask her not to talk about the abuse to anyone who might know my father unless she asks me first. My parents still have acquaintances in common.

"God knows what he'd do if I go public," I say. "Probably nothing. But with all the threats he made to kill us, I don't want to take chances."

<hr />

About an hour after that conversation, my mother calls me back to tell me Margo had telephoned.

"She told me you accused your father of molestation, and the only explanation must be that you're having a nervous breakdown," my mother says. "She asked me to intercede. I refused. I told her I believed *you*, not him. I also told them not to call me again or involve me. If they have something to say, they should deal with you. Then, I hung up. I wanted you to be prepared, in case they call."

I thank her for standing up for me, and smile for the first time in days. Even Margo and my father's actions aren't enough to dampen the satisfaction that seeps in. *I am not only believed. I have an ally.*

<hr />

A couple of days later, my mother is rushed to the hospital with chest pains. After 24 hours of testing, the doctors find nothing. "It must have been stress," they tell her, and send her home. I'm pretty certain the stress is my mother discovering that her ex-husband is a child molester.

I feel some guilt. I've often experienced an insidious fear that my truth hurts others. Now, a little voice says, *See. Better hide out. Stop before anyone else gets hurt. Nobody can handle hearing about incest.* But another louder voice rears up. *No,* it says. *For too long I've carried this secret alone. I need the others involved to carry their share. I won't suffer by myself anymore.*

The photographs of me as a child arrive. With them comes a note from my mother. "I'm so sorry I didn't know," she writes. "If only I had known, our lives would have been different. I would have left your father when you were three. You wouldn't have had to go through what you went through."

Tears well up in my eyes as I read and re-read the note and think about what might have been.

I bring the photos to my next meeting with Sherry. Each one reveals me at ages ranging from three to eleven, standing or sitting in a posed position. "See this innocent child," she says tenderly, pointing at each one. "How could anyone perceive this child as sexual, as someone who should be touched sexually? There's *no* way you somehow asked for it to happen."

I look at the photographs through Sherry's eyes now—searching for the redemption she offers me like a warm cup of tea in a delicate porcelain cup. Slowly, I find it. I find it in the stiff taffeta dress I wore on my third birthday, with its black-and-white checks and full, scratchy petticoat. I find it in my three-year-old arms, extending straight down at my sides. My little fists are clenched. I find it in my kindergarten picture, in my crooked bangs and straight, shoulder-length pale-blond hair, set to curl in a flip, but instead sticking out this way and that. And I find it in my sensitive eyes and closed-mouth smile, lips clamped together to hide various lost teeth.

Finally, drinking in these images of the child I was, I see that I am blameless. I reclaim my innocence. I reclaim my purity. I am at peace.

September 1986

My mother opens her suitcase on the same futon in my bedroom office I've sat on while working through my memories of
abuse during the last four months. Two large photo albums fill
half the available space. "I made these up for you," she says.
"They're of you, from childhood through adulthood. I know I
already sent you some when your therapist suggested it. But I
hoped these would help, too."

A rush of electric energy and emotion sweeps up and down
my spine. Clearly, my mother spent hours putting the albums
together and lugged them on the plane from Chicago where she
now lives. The love of this act touches me. Since childhood,
I've often questioned whether she really loves me, even though
she's spoken the words. How could she and still have allowed
the abuse? This concrete act, in its desire to bring healing, gives
me assurance that she does.

"Mama, that was so sweet," I say, tears welling up, as they
often will over the span of her visit. "You must have spent *days*
putting this together." I hug her tenderly.

Healing is the main reason for her visit, the first since I remembered the abuse. I've asked her to come help fill in some
gaps about it. But we'll be going through this process on our
own rather than in therapy as she offered when I told her about
the incest. About a month before this, when the first wave of
incest issues passed, I no longer felt the need for ongoing counseling support and had stopped seeing Sherry and Philippe.

My mother has also come to help care for me while Jonah
travels to a family wedding. Despite my hopes that remembering the incest would bring physical healing, too, it has upped
my energy by only a small percentage. For the next few days,
like a child again, I must depend on my mother to do tasks I
still can't do on my own, like grocery shopping and driving to
doctor's appointments.

Even before CFS, my mother had more energy than I did.
She still has the stamina of a 25-year-old and looks a dozen

years younger than her true age of 58. Her blond hair, slightly curled under, is cut chin length. Trim and shapely, she is dressed in fitted wrinkle-free blue jeans, a long-sleeved burgundy silk blouse and black pumps. On her finger, she wears a gold Latvian ring with dangling triangle-shaped pieces of gold prevalent on the country's traditional jewelry. Etched into the metal are ancient symbols for good luck. I wear a similar ring in silver that she gave me when I was 15, and a second ring—an amber stone set in a silver sun symbol—that was my grandmother's.

"Come," my mother says, motioning to me. We sit next to each other on the futon, and she opens the first album on our laps. She points to a photo where my father and she hold and gaze at me as an infant. "There's only a couple with your father. He has the rest of the photos of you and him." She pauses. "I remember he'd look at you with such pride when you were a baby." She shakes her head. "And now this."

I feel a tinge of sadness and longing looking at the picture that captured our family in a moment of normalcy—new, doting parents—which would soon be polluted by abuse. Still, as we move on to other photos, I am grateful to be reminded of this childhood that existed side by side with the other childhood that has consumed me these past months. The childhood in these images transcended the abuse and even stretched beyond the clenched fists and stiff poses of the first photos my mother sent. In them, despite what happened, I see that I managed to play, grow, laugh, excel, create, learn, and love.

In one photo, my mother snugly hugs a smiling toddler me as I sit sheltered in her arms at the beach. In another, the eight-year-old me stands with her and my grandparents all decked out in wet rain slickers beneath Niagara Falls. The nine-year-old me hangs upside down from a sidebar on my backyard swing set wearing the new white Easter dress with red trim my mother sewed for me. My hands and arms, at my sides, hold the skirt and petticoat in place so my underpants won't show.

At 10, my best friend Baiba and I march in dark green blouses and pleated skirts, our Girl-Scout uniforms. At 11, I stand on my toes, arms in *port de bras*, transformed into a white unicorn—complete with horn and tail. I'd worn this costume for a ballet recital and when our dance group won a talent contest and performed on TV. The recital program was pasted in the album, too.

"I never knew you saved this," I say appreciatively.

"Oh yes, I have a whole box of things," my mother says. "Report cards. Drawings. Stories and poems you wrote. You had a lot of imagination."

The years of my life pass with the album pages. In high school, I swirl in my fringed drill team outfit. Before the prom, I pose next to my steady boyfriend, hair pulled up and styled, statuesque in a formal blue chiffon dress my mother sewed from a Vogue pattern. Two years later, hair straight and half-way down my back, I wear bell-bottom jeans, a gauze blouse and granny glasses. At 29, standing on a sidewalk in New York City where I worked as a writer, I'm outfitted in arty purple pants and top. My mother lived in New Jersey then, and we often went out to cultural events and restaurants together.

These photos are witnesses, serve as a testament that somehow, despite the abuse, I claimed a full life of my own. I want to hug and tell each resilient girl of me, *"You did it. We made it. Thank you. Thank you."* And as vulnerable as I feel now, as challenging as the illness is, I am also grateful I never have to return to the insanity in that child's life.

Near the end of the second album, my mother has included photos of herself, my grandmother and me, each at 18 years old, to compare how we looked at that age. I stare at my grandmother's serious, wise expression, her single, long braid; my mother's radiant, life-affirming smile and stylish, clipped-back shoulder-length curls; my own shining, expectant eyes and long, loose, straight hair, draping over my shoulders. "Three generations of survivors," I say, thinking of everything my ancestors and I have endured—wars, famine, political oppression, dislocation, abuse. I put my arm around my mother's shoulder. "There's a lot of strength in those faces."

My mother turns her gaze from the photos, looks directly at me. "It wasn't all bad for you, was it?" she asks, tentatively.

"No, Mum, it wasn't," I answer without hesitation, looking back at her. "We did all right." I pause. "I love you, Mamma."

"I love you, too," she responds.

I want to talk about the past in the open air. So the next day, my mother drives us to Palisades Park in Santa Monica. The weather is warm and sunny. We sit on beach chairs on the grass, looking out over cliffs and the Pacific Coast Highway to the ocean. Shade and palm trees surround us. A weekday, the park is relatively empty.

Through numerous discussions about childhood wounding over the past years, my mother and I have already crossed many hurdles and deepened our bond. Now, however, a whole new level of healing is required. Nervous, I take a deep breath and plunge in. I speak mostly in English, the language that lets me speak from my heart. She speaks in Latvian, the language nearest to hers. At first, I ask her to tell me about the abuse she remembers, and she gives shape and substance to even more instances of physical and emotional violence than the ones I'd recollected.

Many emotions pass through the pit of my stomach. Shock. Anger. Sadness. I ask, my voice trembling, "This summer, you wrote you would have left if you'd known about the sexual abuse. But how could you stay witnessing the physical and emotional abuse? I may not remember each incident. But I do remember the terror. Not being protected by you really hurt, and makes me angry even today." Tears flood my eyes. "Why didn't you leave? How could you let him do that?"

"I tried to protect you," she says, looking directly at me, her eyes tearing up, too. "When he went after you, I'd try to put myself between you or change the subject, but that didn't always work. One time, when you were three, he grabbed you before I got to him. He ran into the bedroom, locked the door. I was afraid he'd kill you. I stood on the other side screaming and pounding on the door to let me in, but he wouldn't."

My throat tightens, sensing the panic I must have felt. My

anger rises. "I didn't feel protected. Protecting me would have meant *leaving*. Why didn't you?"

"I didn't see it as an option," she answers, a pained sadness permeating her face. "Women still married for life back then, made the best of the situation. I was only 19 when I married your father. He was already 31. We dated when I was in high school. I had no sense of anything except what he told me about myself. And he told me I was ugly and stupid, that I'd never survive on my own, that no man but him would ever have me. I believed him."

"But you're so beautiful," I say. "How could you believe that?"

"I'd never lived on my own," she says. "I went straight from my family, school, and World War II to your father."

She relates the story I've heard growing up of her wartime experiences. I imagine her as a 13-year-old farm girl in Latvia. One summer night in 1944, she and her family learned that the Russian Front was descending. In 1941, they had already barely missed being deported to Siberia during the first Stalin purge. Several other family members—and tens of thousands of Latvians—had not been so fortunate. In 1944, her family had to leave or face certain deportation—or worse, death. They fled by walking across the country to the Baltic Sea, arriving, after many turns of fate, at a displaced person's camp in Wurtzeburg, Germany. There, my mother and her family lived in a one-room shack until she married my father. A couple years later, they all immigrated to the United States.

But the child in me doesn't care about my mother's challenges growing up. All the child wants to do is scream, "There's *no excuse* for letting him do what he did. I hate you for being so weak. I hate myself for being so weak. How could *you* let *me* feel so weak?" Each thought stabs at my heart. I experience it in my mind as if I were speaking it out loud.

But I silence the child voice that wants to lash out. For now, the adult in me wills her to suspend judgment long enough to hear what I hope will help me reclaim my life. I run the palms of my hands over the grass and feel the bottoms of my feet on the earth to help ground myself. I breathe deeply, imagining that child cradled in the arms of angels.

"The first years, even though he acted crazy, I loved Valdis," my mother says, calling my father by the shortened version of Voldemars she always used. "But, in 1957—we were already in our new house—things got worse. That was when I started working."

My mother had gone to work as a clerk for a Fortune 100 company because my father's paycheck alone didn't cover the increased living expenses at the new house.

"Valdis became more temperamental, began acting out road rage when we were driving together in the car," she says. "If I sat in a place he didn't like at an event, he'd run out and drive off without me. He'd constantly tell me I was a bad cook and tossed food I made into the garbage. He'd say I couldn't clean properly and then re-dust. The only time he was in a good mood was when he was off doing his first love—sports."

"Was he worse with me in the new house, too?" I ask.

"Yes. He became more physically and verbally abusive," she says. "Often, he'd be watching TV in the living room; you'd kiss him good night. For no reason, he'd shove you—hard. You'd fly across the room and end up crumpled on the floor. Then you'd run to your bedroom. But he'd get angry if you didn't say good night to him, too. You had to go back night after night never knowing how he'd react."

"I don't remember a lot of the abuse even now," I say, shaking my head, disconcerted by how much I blocked out.

"Seeing him hurt you hurt me so much," she says. "But I was too afraid to leave. I thought we'd be worse off or he'd hunt us down and kill us."

"Mostly, I recall the stark terror I felt," I say, "especially when you were at work, and he and I were home alone. I remember him getting mad at me, screaming, and storming around the house out of control. Finally, he'd race out; I'd call you at work."

She reaches over to touch my arm. "I remember," she says. "I wanted to run home. But I was afraid of losing my job—which was doing more than paying bills. At work, I had a sense of achievement, of doing something important. At home, I experienced the opposite. I lived two lives."

"I felt the same way about school," I say. "I was appreciated there for my accomplishments and high grades."

My mother nods in recognition. "The biggest conflict for me was when I went to work in Chicago for a few months in 1966," she says. "Away from Valdis, I felt like I was let out of prison. That was the breaking point. His power over me was shattered. I knew I could survive without him."

I think back to that time. I was 15 years old, a sophomore in high school. My mother's company was closing its main office in Cleveland and opening one in Chicago. In return for working on the transition team in Chicago for part of the winter and spring, she was guaranteed a job at the remaining Cleveland office. She only came home on weekends.

I was left completely alone with my father. Mostly, I stayed out of his way, only spending time with him around meals. But, interestingly, with my mother gone, he stopped yelling and sought me out more as a companion than a scapegoat. I didn't trust him though.

Meanwhile, away from my father's critical eye, my mother flourished. She was respected by her bosses and co-workers. She made friends. She experienced a new life. Every night, she ate at gourmet restaurants with colleagues. They attended the opera and ballet and went to art museums.

I was angry she'd left me with my father. Yet I could see her transformation. It was more than her fashionable new haircut, and the shoes and winter coat she purchased from Marshall Field's department store. It was a new vitality in her face and body, a lightness in her voice.

I come back to our conversation in the present. "I know Chicago was good for you, but I can't believe you left me with Papa. I thought he'd kill me. I felt abandoned. I could also tell how much happier you were, and worried you'd never come back. How could you rationalize going away?"

"It was a good job with a good company. I wanted to keep

it," she says. "We needed the money, because your father's job still didn't cover all our living expenses. It also turned out to be the best thing for me. After I returned, I told myself if your father ever hit you again, I'd leave. I hated myself for staying all those years. But for a full year after I came back, I still couldn't get up the courage to leave. Finally, I did leave—because of you."

"How so?" I ask.

She relates an event I recall, too. "The next summer, you and your father were joking around in the kitchen. He pretended to be angry and threw a punch at your face."

"I remember," I say. My father often acted like he was going to slug me, then pulled the punch, hit his own hand right in front of my face instead. It wasn't funny, even though he thought it was. That one time, though, he misgauged the distance and struck me full force on the cheek."

"You started to cry and refused to believe it was an accident," she says. "You accused him of doing it on purpose. He went crazy. He grabbed you by the arms, shook you so hard I thought this time he was going to kill you."

"So did I," I say.

"I screamed at him to stop, but he yelled louder, accused me of always siding with you," she says. "He picked you up by your arms like a sack of potatoes and threw you into the kitchen table and chairs. Everything went flying. You were laying there, lifeless. He rushed out the door, threatening he was going to cut both of our throats like chickens and hang us from our feet until the blood ran out of us."

"I thought he was going to get the axe from the garage and finish us off right then," I say, my heart pounding as I remember.

"I did, too. But instead, he raced away in the car," she says. "Miraculously, you didn't have any broken bones or serious head injuries. But seeing you on the floor—you'd wet your pants you were so scared—I knew I had to leave. That evening, I moved out of our bedroom and into my sewing room. Valdis and I legally separated two months later."

I hadn't remembered wetting my pants. I imagine the shame and horror I felt, feel it now. I also hadn't recalled that this episode was the impetus for my mother's move to the sewing room. But, in this moment, her response seems like too little too late. I feel angry, and want to hold onto that anger.

"How could you stay in the house at all after that?" I say. "How could you keep us in jeopardy?" I realize I'm nervously breaking off blades of grass with my fingers. I stop, and breathe deeply.

"I wish so much I could have," she says. "But if we moved out right away, I was afraid your father would come after us and kill us. I also didn't fully believe I could support us on the salary I was making. I needed time to plan, save a little money and find a place to live."

Ever so slowly, a budding empathy for my mother's position soothes some of the anger I feel. What's most important, I rationalize, is that, ultimately, she did leave. And we both survived. I was 16, had just started my senior year in high school. She was 39.

I remember something else. "You know, oddly enough, when you moved into the sewing room, Papa was nicer to me, like he was when you were in Chicago. The summer before, he'd already started taking me waterskiing. It had actually been enjoyable. Before we moved out, for the first time, he took an interest in me, told me he'd always loved me. He blamed you for us not getting along, and said you turned me against him."

"That's typical," my mother says, "As if I made him abuse you." She shakes her head, pauses for a moment. "Early that fall, I did finally tell Valdis I was leaving. I was sitting on the bed in his room. That day, for the first time, he became physically violent with *me*, too. He shoved me off the bed so hard I was afraid I'd break my neck. I landed right on my elbow and hurt it so badly, it still sometimes bothers me. But nothing he did was going to stop me.

"I had almost no savings. I'd asked for a job transfer with my company to a new state far away from Valdis, but it didn't come through. I couldn't afford to make a move like that on my own. So I rented an apartment for us only a few miles away. Most of the money I saved for the move went into the first month's rent

.and deposit. I kept thinking, *How am I going to do this?* I could hear his voice pounding in my head, saying, *You'll never make it on your own.* But I was also excited to know we were finally going to be free of him."

"Tell me about the nervous breakdown Papa had when we left," I say, beginning to feel tired, but not wanting to stop the conversation. I rub my feet on the grass and imagine energy flowing into me from the earth.

"The first morning in our new apartment, he called, sobbing hysterically and asking me to come back and talk," she says. "When I arrived, he got down on his knees and begged me to come back to him. I tried to leave, but he lost control. Instead of exploding in anger, though, he began to choke and froth at the mouth, as if he was having a fit. At first, I thought he was acting. Then I realized he was gasping for air. He was turning blue, grabbing at his throat.

"I froze and looked at him. There he was, after all those years of brutality, finally helpless, suffocating. I considered all the suffering he had caused you and me. *Let him choke to death*, I thought. *I'd be doing us—and the world—a favor.* I wanted so badly to walk out of the house right then. But I couldn't."

I listen in appreciative amazement, never having heard this part of the story. I knew I'd felt that much anger at my father. But I never knew my mother, who is more emotionally reserved, had tapped that level of rage.

"I called emergency, and they immediately worked with me to get him breathing," she says. "The paramedics arrived minutes later. Our family doctor came, too. He said Valdis was having a nervous breakdown and pumped him full of sedatives. You and I stayed a couple nights. I felt that much responsibility to Valdis and our life together. Then, we left for good."

"He still has breakdowns—though my therapist doubts they're real," I say. "What's weird is that after that first one, I never experienced him being physically abusive or violently losing his temper with me again."

As my mother reveals this most vulnerable moment, she and I are no longer simply mother and child, but two women sharing a common history of coping with and overcoming abuse. For the first time, I fully take in that I wasn't the only person my father abused. Since he wasn't physically violent with my mother until the end of their relationship, I never really perceived her as a survivor of domestic violence. But she was. She dealt with his emotional and verbal violence daily—just like I did. I feel compassion for what she endured, too. My anger recedes a little more.

"Somehow we made it," my mother says. "I used the last of the money I'd saved to buy a dining room set and television/stereo console. Something beautiful and new to celebrate our chance for a new life."

"I remember shopping for that furniture," I say. "I was excited, too."

A look of pleasure permeates her face. In the grass beyond her, I notice finches with orange-red throats, like those I feed outside my apartment. I never knew how to recognize a finch until I became ill and bought a book to identify the ones I fed with birdseed every day.

"To make sure we had enough money, I took on extra work," she continues. "Besides my job, I started doing custom sewing for some women in the apartment complex. Your father had hired a high-priced divorce lawyer, so I got nothing from him, not even from the house we paid for together. Only the down payment my parents had lent us. I insisted he pay it back to them. I was still such a silly goose about money. All I wanted was to get away."

"Even his wife, Margo, agrees. She told me what he did wasn't right," I say.

"But that's all in the past," she says. "I was glad to be on my own. And you and I had some good times living away from him in that apartment. Remember when we got into gourmet cooking and made things like strawberry soufflé with Grand Marnier and beef fondue with all those dipping sauces?"

I nod. For a moment, I see us back in our small kitchen, experimenting, cooking, laughing out loud in a way we never did living with my father.

"I remember before I left your father, my divorce lawyer asked, 'Do you know how long you'll be single if you leave?'" my mother says, brushing her hair back from her face. "I told him, 'Forever. But that's okay. I'd rather be alone.' He burst out laughing. 'Not a chance. A woman as beautiful and charming as you will remarry in 18 months.' I was so shocked. I began to see myself in a new way and thought maybe some day I could have a relationship again. But I also wasn't in a rush. I was never going to let another man do what your father did to me. And I haven't."

"No, you've taken care of yourself and encouraged me to do the same," I say.

"When I left, I needed to rebuild my confidence though," she says. "I remember the first time I went to a formal dance without a date. It was part of a cultural festival. Most of the night, I sat—in the beautiful, long gown I'd sewn for myself—in a bathroom toilet stall. I tried to work up the courage to come out. But I was too terrified." She shakes her head. "I've come a long way."

And she has. In fact, she's danced at many festivals and created a network of friends all over the world. She's traveled by herself throughout Europe. She's risen up the ranks of the Fortune 100 company she's worked at for nearly 30 years to become a financial analyst. She's owned homes and created financial security. She's been in a committed relationship for the last 10 years. But she never married again.

"What I'm still sorry for is what happened to you, Vita," she says. "For all of it. For how hard this has been on you. I'm sorry I didn't protect you well enough. I'm sorry you were afraid. What I did, I did out of love for you. When you were little, I had no idea how to be a mother, and I had no one to turn to for help. Then, I was so beaten down emotionally by Valdis. I did the best I could. I wish I could have done better."

As she talks, I see my mother as the girl and young woman who lived through trauma herself, the single mother who created a fulfilling life and made sure I got an education, all peering at me through her now middle-aged face. Once more,

I feel compassion rising for how helpless she had felt in her marriage, for how much she overcame. I also hear her taking some responsibility for what occurred.

Tears fill her eyes. I reach over to touch her shoulder. We spontaneously hug. Tears come for both of us, sweet tears of release. In this moment, the anger I felt toward her dissolves. I forgive her.

The rest of our visit, the discussion turns away from our family dynamics. We sit on the couch talking about the illness, about a TV program she watched about sexual abuse survivors. She shares highlights of a trip she took. We eat Chinese take-out. When I'm too tired to talk, we watch old movies on the VCR. We hold hands while Audrey Hepburn and Gary Cooper mesmerize each other in *Love in the Afternoon*.

My mother gently scratches my back, like she did when I was a girl. For a moment, I am transported to my childhood. Backrubs were my favorite part of our daily ritual. My mother would come into my bedroom, sit down on the edge of my bed and ask me about my day. I would get under the covers, and she scratched my back to help me fall sleep.

I hoped those times would go on forever. The loving touch. The closeness. I'd lie as still as possible, barely breathing, not wanting any movement to remind my mother she had to get on with her evening chores. As she scratched, instinctively knowing the right pressure to use, I felt her love the most. It was as if she transmitted it electrically through her fingers. I drank it in, soaked it in. Those back scratches were as important to me as food.

Even now that I'm an adult, occasionally, when we're relaxing together during a visit, usually while watching TV, she'll reach over, rub and scratch my back. Today, after she finishes, I gently scratch her back in return.

Standing My Ground

August 1987

About a year after my mother's visit, a letter arrives from my father, our first contact since the phone call about sexual abuse. Home alone, I sit on the rust-colored couch and open it. The handwriting is Margo's; the words are my father's. Because of his difficulty with English, he explains, he wants to make sure I understand what he has to say.

After my "horrible accusation," he suffered for two whole weeks, he writes, and was too upset to touch Margo for fear she'd also accuse him of abusing her. He hoped by this time, I would have come to my senses. A doctor must have planted the idea in my head, because I couldn't make this up on my own. I should get away from the doctor who "screwed up" my mind.

He concocts this story: He tells me that at age three, I went to visit Tony and Sophia, a neighbor couple who had befriended me. Afterward, I stated I'd never go there again and refused to tell my father why. Tony must have taken advantage of me, but the blame fell back on my father.

I used to watch TV at their apartment, he says. To ensure his "little girl" could still watch her favorite programs, the very next day, he and my mother bought a TV—a big expense for them. Drop your allegations so we can be a family again, he writes. Throughout the letter, he never once uses the words *incest, sexual abuse,* or *molestation*.

My immediate response is anger. Anger he still doesn't admit what he did. Anger at his attempt to deflect responsibility, as usual. Anger that the loss of his only daughter, not to mention the reason he lost me, was only worth *two weeks* of suffering.

I had suffered exponentially more than two weeks as a result of the abuse and continued to suffer. And now, for nearly two years, I'd also been swept up in the pain of dealing with a debilitating illness, which very likely resulted from the lingering jolt of the abuse in my body. How could my father get away with only two uncomfortable weeks? Even more enraging, how could he be walking around free, vibrantly healthy, traveling, actively living his life, loved by his wife?

I call my mother. "He's lying—trying to look good for his wife again," she says. "You went to see Tony and Sophia daily. They loved you. When you were five, we were still so close to them, we took apartments right next to each other in another apartment building in the suburbs. You only stopped seeing them regularly when we moved to our new house. Then, we lived too far away."

"That's what I remember, too," I say. "Their place was a safe haven for me. What about the television?"

"Another lie," she says. "Valdis bought it for himself. You were only allowed to watch your programs when he wasn't home. Are you going to answer the letter?"

"Well, I don't want to talk to him again," I say, "But I will write back. I'm not sure yet what I'll say, other than to call him on the lies."

Each day, I expend my limited concentration in short stints of writing what will turn into a 10-page, single-spaced letter to my father. I begin by stating that eight years of incest was my reality, remembered and relived, painful detail by painful detail. It was not a fantasy concocted by a doctor, and not only one incident when I was three. Tony's face was not the one I saw molesting me. It was my father's. I divulge my memories, and how I've suffered so immeasurably much more than two weeks. I bring up the possibility that he himself blocked out the incest and suggest he see a therapist. I ask him to take responsibility and apologize. In the end, I wish him and Margo healing, tell him this is now between him and God. I wish it because while I see the need for consequences for what he did to me, I also recognize the need for healing—for him and for all abusers in the world—as much as for myself and for all other survivors of abuse.

I put the letter away for two weeks—to make certain I haven't forgotten anything and will still want to mail it. I do. Not because I believe it will move my father to confess. He probably won't even read it. First and foremost, I send it for myself. I send it to own and speak my truth even more than I've already done. I send it to tell him all I've remembered and experienced since our phone call. I send it because it's important to me to put forth in my own words that I know he is culpable, and that I want an admission, an apology, atonement. I send it because regardless of how or if my father responds, I still feel that this is what I need to do for further release and healing. It's not about what he will or won't do in response. I can't make him do anything. It's about reverberating my truth in his presence, sounding it out in my own being, of not backing down, of saying "No more. You can't intimidate me into submission, or hiding, or silence, anymore."

Because even if he doesn't read the letter, even if I never know his response to the words I write, I know the very act of sending this letter itself creates a shift, an opening. I claim my power in a way that has nothing to do with him, but everything to do with my willingness to take this step. I heal myself and invite my father to join me in the process. What's most crucial is that I send the letter for me. How he reacts is his responsibility.

I drive the letter to a mailbox a few blocks away, because the illness still prevents me from walking this far. The mailbox stands at the corner of a tree-lined side street, with rows of mostly smaller two-and three-story stucco apartment buildings on either side. Just before 10 a.m., slight lulls appear in the normally endless traffic. The weather is standard Los Angeles—sunny, 75 degrees.

I face the mailbox, lower its door. A nervous flutter of butterflies in my stomach transforms into a pelting rain of fear. My heart pounds so loudly in my ears it drowns out the noise of the intermittent stream of passing cars. The only other sound is the voice of that fear in my head. *He'll kill you if you tell*, it says. I acknowledge the voice, drop the letter in the box anyway. I stand back, breathe deeply and take in what I've done and cannot undo without committing a federal crime. The terror slowly subsides.

What slips into its place, though, is not the sense of accomplishment, power, or courage I expect, but a shroud of grief. I feel like I've just watched my father's coffin being lowered into the ground. Only instead of black mourning, I'm wearing a faded green shirt, loose beige pants, and sneakers. More shocking is that I care. Staring at the mailbox, shoulders heaving, strands of dark blond, permed hair stuck to my face by tears, I weep in broad daylight. I don't even care how certifiable I must look to passersby.

Over the next few weeks, I continue to grieve—for myself, for him, for my mother, for my ancestors. I grieve the abuse and loss we all endured. I grieve for everyone who was or still is being abused. I also mourn the loss of the potential for love and admission that won't be. All my life, I craved my father's love and acceptance. No matter how disturbed he was, inside me lived a gaping wound yearning to be filled by that love. And, like so many people who grew up in a dysfunctional family, nothing I recalled before the incest quelled that longing. Not even being conscious of how useless it was or of how incapable he was of giving that love. As a child, it felt like a matter of life and death whether or not I received it.

When I think back to my childhood, I remember how even a glimmer of a promise of caring returned was all I needed to open my heart to the very parent who'd repeatedly hurt and rejected me. Despite his abusiveness. Despite my fear of him and the anger that seethed silently inside me.

Mostly, my heart had opened to him for the hours we spent swimming and waterskiing. During those times engaged in the sports he most loved, it was as if he was temporarily released from the demons that haunted him, and we abided by an un-spoken truce. As I entered my late teens and twenties, the truce gradually extended to apply when we were on land, too. After he and my mother divorced, he stopped being abusive to me and even expressed some caring. When he and Margo got mar-ried, her sunny presence and kindness served to create a buffer between my father and me, and we developed even more of a relationship. I never saw him abuse her.

Our truce only lasted into my late twenties, however. When I went into therapy and began to delve into my feelings about the physical and emotional abuse I already remembered, my father's and my relationship grew increasingly rocky. I recog-nized his narcissism more and was less willing to tiptoe around his neuroses. Once, when I broached the subject of the past, we argued, and he didn't talk to me for a year. By the time I was in my early thirties, I had difficulty spending more than a couple of hours at a time with him.

Now in the present, since I've remembered the incest and mailed my response to his letter, even the rocky relationship I had with my father is gone. And as the weeks pass, I take in fully the fact that all my work over the course of my life—to learn to love him, to look for what good there was in him, to maintain a connection with him—has come to this painful truth.

He will not come to his senses. He will not call me, wracked by guilt, to confess and apologize. I will not ever experience anything but the conditional caring that masqueraded as his love. I will not be acknowledged by him or accepted for who I am. One of my parents is lost. The love I once felt for him is lost, too. Aching emptiness remains where love once resided.

December 1987

During the first two years of my search for healing the CFS and abuse, I read about the mind-body connection and many people's spiritual and shamanic healing paths—amongst others, books by Lynn Andrews, Alberto Villoldo, Jean Houston, Joan Halifax, Jeanne Achterberg, Shirley MacLaine, and Edgar Cayce. The one that affects me most profoundly is *Autobiography of a Yogi* by Paramahansa Yogananda, an enlightened Hindu master.

What he experiences on his own road to enlightenment expands my perceptions of the many realms of existence. Yogananda writes about healing from a terminal illness in an instant; people dematerializing and re-materializing again; people bi-locating—being viewed in more than one location at the same time; and other such extraordinary occurrences. In India, miracles exist on a daily basis, and are an accepted part of life. This opens me more to the possibility that first resounded when I worked with Philippe, the energy healer who helped me recover the abuse memories: the possibility that I, too, can truly have miracles of healing, that divine grace can cure my body, and heal the wounds of the past.

Meanwhile, with the two-year anniversary of my encounter with CFS approaching, there's nary a miracle of healing in sight. Even after writing the letter to my father and letting myself grieve the losses in my life, my symptoms have not abated. True, with all the emotional and spiritual work I do, I have developed greater courage and faith than before; had deep insights about abuse and illness; and learned lessons about love, compassion, surrender, and living in the now. True, with all the alternative therapies I try—from specialized homeopathy to acupuncture and Chinese herbs—I may feel better and be able to do more than people who are bed-ridden for years with the illness. But, overall, I still slog through the gray zone—my activity and physical well-being greatly limited, feeling humbled and discouraged in the face of this disease.

One night, during this period, I dream about Babaji, a Hindu avatar whom Yogananda writes about in his autobiography. For hundreds of years, Babaji has chosen to remain in human form. Becoming invisible at will, he appears only occasionally to impart spiritual wisdom and aid the progress of humans. This deathless guru from the Himalayas never ages, always looking about 25 years old with long, copper-colored hair, dark eyes, and a strong body.

In my dream, a group of drug addicts line up. Babaji ministers to them. Their skin pallor gray, they stand, shoulders and heads hunched forward, unable to relate even to each other. Babaji tells them that he is going to give them each a shot to euthanize them. Dying under his guidance, he explains, will release the karmic debt they collected as a result of their addiction and drug-related activities. When they reincarnate into their next life, they will start with a fresh karmic slate, cleansed and new.

He looks at me. "Even though you're not an addict, you need to be euthanized and start over, too," he says, and directs me to the end of the line. Without hesitation, I trust what he says and agree. My turn comes. I feel the prick of the needle entering my arm. Immediately, sinking into unconsciousness, I perceive the white light I've read people witness during near-death experiences, the light that represents Divine Love Itself. I let go, and without resistance, open my arms and heart wide, surrender to it. The Love permeates every cell of my being. I experience pure bliss.

Babaji whispers softly in my ear, his voice sounding as if it is comes from a great distance. "Do you want to live?" he murmurs.

And without thought, without regard for the strong pull to remain with the exquisite love, from the depths of my being emerges, "Yes. I want to live. I want to live."

Suddenly, I am back in my body, no longer dying, no longer unconscious, fully awake and alive, Babaji beside me. He explains that this was a spiritual test, not euthanasia at all. That now, I have fully chosen life. If I hadn't wanted to live, he would have given me a second shot and let me go to spirit.

I wake up in my own bed, in the dark of night, sobbing, filled with that same desire and choice, repeating the phrase, "I want to live. I want to live. Despite CFS. Despite sexual abuse. I want to live."

Over the coming weeks, I become aware that the profundity of the choice I made with Babaji has opened me to value and accept life more fully, just as it is, moment by moment, even with the severe limitations of illness. At the same time, with the infusion of life force that comes from making this choice, I'm more motivated than ever to do what's necessary to heal my body and the remaining wounds of abuse.

Allopathic medicine still offers little encouragement. The conventional approach to dealing with CFS says that I should simply submit to allopathic medicine's bleak prognosis: CFS has no cure. It can at best be eased symptomatically—with drugs. All I can do is rest (for years), do very limited exercise, maintain a positive attitude (with the aid of antidepressants) and wait to get over it—maybe—because many don't. I can passively hang on until a few brave researchers, working with minimal dollars, find the cause and cure for CFS.

The alternative medicine I've tried has offered me more hope. Its more varied options have given me some symptomatic relief, more active engagement in my own emotional and physical healing process, and the possibility of ultimately finding the right combination of methods, herbs, nutritional supplements, and mind-body connection to bring healing. But while I plan to continue down this road, I'm also sorely aware that I've already been traveling it for nearly two years, without arriving at any destination.

That brings me back to miracles. I'm no longer satisfied only reading about them, I realize, and believing in the miracles that happen to other people. A voice rises up in me, first barely a whisper, gradually ringing out to the universe. It says, "I want a miracle myself," and even more forcefully, "I can and *will* have a miracle. And I am willing to consciously and actively do whatever I need to do to open to that miracle."

Claiming a miracle for my own life in this way seems right in alignment with the kind of passion for life that screamed out from my depths, *"I want to live,"* in the Babaji dream. It grounds me like the powerful vibration of a Japanese Taiko drumbeat, reverberating up through my hands and arms, filling my body with resonance.

And as if on cue, even as I am still wondering how to find

a good spiritual and energy healer, I hear about some from friends and acquaintances. These are healers who have witnessed and participated in miracles and spontaneous healings of disease and emotional wounding firsthand. I begin to work with them.

They caution that I am not to look at *them* as the healers. I am my *own* healer—not them. And that we all work in co-creation with the Divine, the greatest healer of all. They also teach me the techniques to do the energy work on myself, processes meant to clear away emotional and physical obstacles, deal with lingering abuse issues, and bring the infusion of light and love that can result in a full healing.

I learn to energetically "blow up" abuse memory pictures, effectively discharging their negative impact. I learn about the power of intention, about visualizing health—walking health, talking it, dancing it—acting "as if" I'm healthy, even if only in my imagination. I learn processes like energy grounding, chakra clearing, energy grid repairing, energy protection, past-life regression, and opening more to my intuition and psychic ability for guidance. I meet my first spirit guides, Mattie and Elizabeth, both master healers, who come to assist me with my creative writing and self-healing.

These methods seem not only to help reduce symptom flare-ups, but they stimulate me and add new dimension to my life. They help me see the larger perspective of illness and abuse. They empower me at a time when I sorely need empowerment.

Science—physics—has already revealed to us that we're all energy, not matter. But now I'm living that wisdom by consciously working with that energy. As I learn to direct my own divine symphony of energy and healing, I also integrate more fully that miracles of some kind are not only possible, but probable. Even inevitable. And not only for me, but for everyone.

With these approaches, I enter a whole new way of being in the world. But this new path is not only about, "Poof, magic, you're healed. End of story." In truth, it's not even about knowing and following the specific energy techniques I learn. Ultimately, the healing facilitators and I recognize that healing from CFS and abuse, healing from any major illness or challenge, is not about a quick body or mind fix that lets me get back to business as usual. Instead, I accept more and more that true healing, the true miracle I seek, comes from opening to and heeding the deepest calling of my soul. In its most genuine sense, it comes from transforming my life, from opening to my authentic nature—and everyone else's—which is love. That may or may not involve a physical healing. Still, I continue to want that healing and to believe I will have it.

One event in particular from this time period echoes the possibility of that healing, like a blast of light showing the way through the dark of a tunnel.

On a cool, rainy day in mid-February, I wake up feeling achy and brain-fogged. Normally, I'd zombie out on the couch for the duration, catch up on some afternoon TV. Instead, a clear voice in my muddled head says, "Don't let the virus get the better of you today. Regardless of how you physically feel, feel good about yourself. Be thankful for where you are now. And believe fully in your ability to self heal."

I forego the couch and settle in on the blue futon in my office, where I generally meditate, write in my journal, and do my self-healing work. For two hours straight, I engage in the healing processes I've recently learned. And I not only visualize and pray for health, I insist upon it. Every fiber of my being wakes up, transforms into a wave of focused intent rippling out to the universe, to the Divine.

Abruptly, the energy in the room shifts. My heart pounds, but strangely, I feel no fear. A golden light materializes before me in the room, like the soft glow of a Japanese lantern against the blue-black sky of twilight. It moves toward me. I "hear" in my mind that the light is the Archangel Raphael, the angel of healing. He wants to merge with me. Without words, without question, I simply grasp that what is happening is *real*. It's like I've been waiting for him for so long, without even realizing I was waiting, like I've known him for a such a long time, only

I've forgotten, *forgotten*. Like I've been living a dream—until this very moment of awakening.

And here he is. A-h-h, *that* angel. My angel. Everyone's angel. *I recognize him.*

And I remember. And I remember that I've always remembered.

No need for explanations. No need for words. No need for boundaries.

An Archangel has dropped by on a rainy afternoon, and his coming feels as natural as the coming of a deep soul brother lost to me for eons and lifetimes who unexpectedly shows up one day for tea. Only he brings me the chalice already filled with drink instead. A drink of Divine Love. And it's as if I've been delirious on the desert for I can't recall how long, and my parched soul is drinking in, drinking in Divine Love through every opening and pore, my face, body submerged in a pool on an oasis.

With certainty, I open to Raphael, to the pool, and am slaked by an all-encompassing, absolute love, unlike any human love I've known. I'm stroked by it, stoked by its liquid turned to cleansing fire. Enveloped by liquid love flame, I cry unabashedly—tears not of sadness, but of the release that comes from being touched by grace.

This Divine Love with Its all-understanding, all-seeing intelligence knows everything about me, I sense—from the basest to the most exalted. And It still loves me—without condition, whether or not I believe I deserve it, without even asking for anything in return. It loves me regardless of what I've done or not done, what I've thought or not thought, what I've accomplished or not. It loves me whether I'm good enough or not good enough, and without any judgment, right or wrong, over what happened to me in the past. This Infinite Love sees everything in me—deed, memory, hope, dream—and loves me for eternity. Nothing I do or say can make It stop Its pure outpouring of love and acceptance. My insatiable thirst finally quenched, my heart opens petal by petal, a bud coming into full bloom as I join in sacred union with this love that connects me to the oneness of all life.

This merging with Divine Love, this meeting with Raphael, a miracle in itself, seems to happen outside of time. As it occurs, I have no idea whether one minute or a full day has passed. Later I realize it lasted for an hour.

What comes is a bounty of healing. On that day, I experience the first major sustained shift in energy since I became ill. While the physical healing that comes isn't total, two years and two months into the illness, I celebrate finally emerging out of the gray zone, out of the monotone of disease limitations, and rediscovering multi-hued shades of color in my life.

But perhaps even more profound than the physical shift is the emotional and spiritual one. Receiving Raphael's gift of Divine Love brings healing to the place in me that felt so tainted, so marked, so wounded by the abuse, and now by illness, that it has always questioned whether or not I am even worthy of love, that has doubted even when I've been surrounded by humans who openly express their love for me. The profound healing also shows me that this love is always available, not just for me on this one day, but for all people, murderer, saint, and everyone in between. Love is even available—and this is a big gulp for me—for my father. And when I sink into this understanding, I feel such tender mercy. Such sweet gratitude.

I am loveable. We are all lovable. The Divine loves us. Even if every human we know disappears, dies, leaves, betrays, or rejects us, even if our dog hates us, we are loved. The Divine is with us. The Divine is with me. And while my ego may forget this again and again—while my ego may at times balk at my father and others of his ilk being loved like this, too—at my core remains only this wholeness, only this truth, only this love.

A boundless peace washes over me. And, in this moment, with a full certainty that I am loved, I also know that one day I will be completely healed from the CFS and any remaining wounds of sexual abuse. And, regardless of what the healing looks like from the outside, it will actually be this Love that visited today that heals me. This knowingness will help sustain me many times through the remaining years of healing from this illness.

For several days, the cooling waters of Divine Love follow me as I open with joy and gratitude to a greater, though still limited, capacity for outer life participation. I can't work or do the creative writing that I love yet, but with pacing, I see and talk to friends more often, drive myself to appointments, go to the park. I take short walks again and shop in the grocery store. I become more active with a service group that Jonah and I helped create.

Small things—maybe—to the average person, my pre-illness self included. But these very things bring the meaning and texture and balance that help sustain me through the weeks and months and years. These are things that before CFS, I so often brushed by as I raced through the days. How rarely did I fully appreciate the joy of simple acts, like picking out my own produce at the health food store and acknowledging all that went into getting that produce there in the first place. I never take these acts for granted again.

With the perspective of my encounter with Divine Love buoying me, I also begin to appreciate that—even if I'm never able to write creatively again—my single greatest creative expression, my highest achievement, is the way I live my life and approach my healing each day. Living as fully and meaningfully as possible with CFS, healing from the horror of incest, opening to the love at my center and to the Divine within me—these endeavors truly do take tremendous imagination and inventiveness. I come to see my life as my truest work of art. At its core are not any of the identities with which I've defined myself in the past. Not the "I am a writer" or "I am this or that." Not even "I am a person with CFS and an incest survivor." But simply *"I am."*

Learning to Fly

May 1990

Four years since remembering the abuse and four and a half years since CFS entered my life.

Over time, I recognize that dealing with a chronic illness, like CFS, and with the wounds of abuse, is like taking the classic hero/heroine's journey that Joseph Campbell describes so eloquently. My own spiritual odyssey comes complete with an extended period of testing and aid from both human and spirit helpers.

The journey rips away my old life foundation and hints at a new one. It demands that I see life in a fresh way, respond to the reverberating call of the universe to pay attention, to change, to grow and evolve. Here, I'm not a victim of my father or an illness. Instead, I recreate myself as an explorer of consciousness and soul awareness, an alchemist transmuting darkness into light, an initiate mastering the art of co-creation with the Divine.

Yes, the ego first wants to stay put—even if it's suffering. Yes, there are uncomfortable, even terrifying trials along the way. As I stumble from this path to that, some healing modalities turn out to be mistakes, a waste of money. Others bring on unnerving healing crises that offer up only more pain, instead of the physical improvements they promise. But I know in my heart of hearts and soul of souls that this direction is where when I slip and fall, I get to laugh with myself and clean off my scrapes. Even if I'm sometimes the fool, I also discover the gold.

Here, I open to myself, my soul purpose, and my true connection to Spirit. I heal the wounds of abuse and the root of the illness—not only for myself, but, in some way I don't fully comprehend, for my family as well. Ultimately, I get to dance in the light—even if my body remains stationary—and maybe even hold up the light for others to see. This is the grand potential, the up-side of a life-changing event, like abuse or illness.

Four years into my healing odyssey, still having only about 25 percent of my pre-CFS capacity and energy, I ride out pages' worth of symptoms daily. Some days and weeks are better. Others, I'm completely laid up. I've recovered enough, though, that I bring in some income, writing articles part-time from home.

My progress is still visible primarily as greater emotional and spiritual well-being, rather than as any radical physical shift. In terms of healing abuse patterns, it also reveals itself notably in my dream life.

When I first remembered the abuse, my father would appear in my dreams, grabbing at my breasts or crotch. I'd be trapped, unable to get away from him. Now, even though I often still live in the same house with him in my dream life, I plan to move out. When he makes advances, I escape and call for help.

Around the fourth anniversary of remembering the incest, a single dream transforms my life. That day, in real time, Jonah accidentally breaks a crystal vase, one of my only possessions from childhood, a confirmation gift from a friend of my father's. It survived all my moves back and forth across the country. Now, it's shattered.

I have this dream: *Jonah and I go to my childhood home where my father lives with his present wife, Margo. We steal his crystal*

vase, because I feel he owes me for all I suffered at his hand. Soon,
however, I regret the theft, and decide Jonah should sneak inside and
return it.

First, I wait outside the house, then slip inside to look for Jonah.
I can't find him. Too afraid to remain there alone, I start to tiptoe
out again, but mistakenly slam a door in the process. My father and
Margo run in, discovering me. He is angry, and I feel sorry for what
I have done. I apologize, telling him why I am there. "I never meant
to shock you like this or hurt you by sneaking in," I say. "What I did
was wrong, but I never intended for you to see me."

He relaxes and says gently," Since you're here, maybe we should
try to begin to communicate."

I feel myself melting, softening toward him, too. I agree. As I do,
both of us are overwhelmed by love. He reaches out and hugs me. I
hug him back, and for a moment, I surrender to the love between us.
But an alarm goes off inside my head. I pull back, saying, "I feel so
good that the line of communication is open. I want to talk, but this
is too much too soon." He accepts this.

"Finally," Margo says. "It's about time."

When I wake up, the warmth and intense love continue. I
cry tears of happiness and sweet release at the dream healing.
Up until this moment, wanting to meet my father again has not
even crossed my mind.

The very next night, I dream of him again. Once more, he,
Jonah, Margo, and I have a blissful encounter. All is healed. My
father and I hug. And this time, I feel only warmth, love—no
pulling back.

In the light of day, however, I feel disconcerted. While the
dreams point to forgiveness and reconciliation, they are also
dreams. Awake, I don't love my father anymore. And that kind
of healing, with the man who won't even admit that he abused
and raped me, seems impossible.

Over the years, many of my healing practitioners have
broached forgiveness. Forgive, not for him, they say, but for
yourself, so that you can drop any ties to him. Your anger keeps
you bound.

Yet whenever anyone mentioned forgiveness, my muscles

hardened to steel. Mother, yes. But father? Doing this, the healers coaxed, might unblock stuck energy, tap it for healing my
body, mind, and spirit. This possibility tempted me for sure,
but still I resisted. While I'd processed garbage barges of anger
at him and unearthed some compassion for his personal suffering, I couldn't fathom forgiving him.

"Maybe in the future it will become a goal," I said. "For
now, I'm not ready. And I don't believe that my physical and
emotional healing—or anyone else's for that matter—requires
forgiving a sexual abuser."

However, even as my conscious will resists, the shifting begun in the dreams insinuates itself into my waking life. About a
week later, in meditation, an image of my father comes unbid-
den to my mind's eye. He stands before me, drops to his knees,
and bows his head in submission. Humbly and peacefully, he
asks for my forgiveness. Shocked, resisting, I don't want to
forgive. Not even in this drama playing itself out on the movie
screen of my mind. Without waiting for a response, my father
rises and offers me a ball of light. "This ball represents the life
and love I couldn't express to you during our life together," he
says. "It's my new legacy to you—the opportunity to express
love and live fully in your own life now."

I hesitate, but my intuition says to take it. When I do, my
father crumbles to ashes. I place them in an urn and throw it
into the cosmic ocean. There, the evil and dysfunction of his
life vanish. Only his purified soul of love remains, the Divine
within him—the Divine within each one of us. This is what's
released and freed into the universe. What also lingers is my
own enhanced understanding that love heals and transmutes
even the greatest darkness.

Afterward, I still don't know what this all means in my day-
to-day life. In my eyes-open reality, physical discomfort reigns
supreme. My father does not show up at my door admitting his
culpability. And I have not forgiven him.

The very next weekend, Jonah and I hear Ram Dass, a well-
known spiritual teacher, speak about caregiving for his father,
who had recently died. He stresses the need for us to love every-

one, even those we have every reason to hate, and the need to speak the truth to each other, even when painful.

A meditation he guides us through deepens those messages. As in my dreams, I melt with love and forgiveness for my own father. And this time, when I open my eyes, the feelings no longer disappear. They're part of me now. Surrendering to them, I'm also finally clear about what to do with them.

I write my father a letter saying that I forgive him and want to see him, to at least begin the process of healing the past—even if he can't admit the incest. I wait 14 days to give myself a chance to change my mind, then send the letter.

Within a week, on July 9th, 1990, my father writes back, refusing my request. No one can remember anything from when they were three years old, he states. Living happily with Margo, he doesn't want himself or Margo to be hurt anymore. He'll only see me if I take back my original accusation and agree never to mention it again.

I am momentarily stunned to see this precious offering of forgiveness and reconciliation back in my own hands, rejected. I certainly can't agree to his conditions. But surprisingly, rather than closing, my heart remains as deep and wide as the ocean. And over the next days, this expansiveness and the love I still feel inspire waves of energy and movement inside me. It feels like I'm tapping into the power of the ocean itself.

I sense that these waves are the opening of energy in my body and spirit—just as the healers who'd initially suggested forgiveness said I might experience once I forgave him. This kind of opening could lead not only to healing of mind and spirit, but to physical healing as well. Even though I still don't believe I *had* to forgive in order to invite healing, I am grateful for the potential that seems to have opened up. I decide to pursue a full-on healing now with greater intention and focus.

At the time, Jonah and I are house-sitting for a week for a friend who lives in a spacious, airy, sunlit house, which looks out over Santa Monica Canyon all the way to the ocean. Each day, I go downstairs to the family room and sit on the floor propped up by pillows against a door. Through the windows, I see the reddish-brown stone deck and a tiered garden, unruly with flowers in shades of soft pastels. I claim a sacred space there by lighting a candle and placing it in front of me, along with a piece of unpolished rose quartz to increase the frequency of love and a double-terminated crystal to intensify the divine light energy. For one to two hours each day, I call out to the Divine and ask for a healing.

Afterward, I close my eyes to meditate and I open to whatever will come. Feelings of forgiveness for my father arise once again, still arriving easily and unrestricted.

And then I surrender myself to the power of that ocean inside me, like I might surrender to the sounds of crashing surf, when I stand on the shore at a physical ocean's edge. I let the surf inside me, endlessly chanting its ocean mantra, slowly empty all thoughts, even of forgiveness, from my mind.

The ocean energy draws me in quickly now, past the first shock-me-awake ice-cold water, past the first heady smells of salt and seaweed, beckoning me deeper with waters that radiate healing all the way down to my cells. Without my even being aware of it, I'm soon in over my head, out past the first set of breaker waves, out in the ocean where surfers would wait to catch a ride, if there were any. But I'm not afraid. I wait, alone, bobbing and trusting. Many waves pass. Then "the" wave comes. And even though I don't know what I'm doing or why it's "the one," even though I don't have a board or know how to ride, I know that this is the wave I must take. Now.

So I consciously take the wave, rise up on it, shift my weight back and forth to find a balance between surrendering to it and riding it with single-minded, focused purpose.

I visualize health on all levels—body, mind, and spirit.

Over the next four days, I ride, head up, ocean winds joining ocean surf in clearing my mind of all I've ever known as possible. Arms out at my sides to steady myself. . .

I see myself as already whole and healthy.

Knees bent, adjusting my stance. . .

I practice the healing processes the healers have taught me.

Synchronizing my whole being with that of the wave, of the ocean. . .

I let go to the vastness inside me.

Infused with the unabashed joy of co-creating with the ocean, the healing salt spray of ocean water, and sun on body, washing and warming away ancient sorrows of the heart. . .

I embrace the deeper love, peace, and compassion that emerge for my father and all beings.

On the fifth day, July 14th, Bastille Day, Liberation Day, others join me on the wave. My spirit guides. Elizabeth, Mattie, each take a hand, and I yield even more, until all three of us become one. Before me, I see an expanse of shimmering light, palpable, tangible light. We ride the wave right into it, through it. I relax, and the light lifts me up and beyond the wave, beyond the guides.

It is the Archangel Raphael. He has returned. My beloved angel. Everyone's angel. Raphael. All around me and through me. My beloved. Bowing to me, he honors me for opening my heart to forgiveness of what seems unforgivable, and for all I have learned on this journey through illness and abuse. He graces me once more with his healing love.

Surrendering to it, matching it with my own, we somersault through a starry night.

Yes to love.

Waft like the scent of lush wildflowers through a fresh green spring meadow.

Yes to release.

Fly through the canopy of a primordial redwood forest, cool green leaves glancing across my skin.

Yes to healing.

Merge with a triple rainbow arcing across a valley.

Yes to miracles.

Give birth to a sliver of a crescent moon, tenderly place it in the early morning sky just before dawn.

Yes to new life. Yes. Yes.

Out of the ocean, I stand back on the shore now, facing inland, my feet adjusting to contact with beach, to the sand beneath them, after riding on water for so long. Behind me, waves roll in, one by one by one, as they have for earth's lifetime, tide ebbing and flowing.

And all my symptoms are gone. And I am healed.

Afterward, before I've told Jonah that my energy and health have returned, that I'm symptom-free, he gazes at me. "That look on your face. I've never seen it. It's like compassionate wisdom, with a depth beyond anything I've ever noticed there before. It's like your soul is on your face."

Such foot-stomping joy we share with each other as I reveal what's transpired. Holding hands, we jump up and down, squealing, whooping it up like a baseball team that just won the World Series. We throw our arms around each other, tears of delight running down our faces, deep laughter rising up from our bellies and overtaking us. More elation fills us as the week unfolds, and I notice that I no longer have to weigh every action or activity to see if I have the energy and mental clarity to participate.

As I pick up the phone to call and tell my mother, my friends, I fling off a burden I didn't even know had weighed me down these last years—the burden of so often being the bearer of painful news, news that would bring sorrow to those I loved. What soul-nourishing bliss for me instead to be able to fly them to the moon as I begin each conversation, "I have incredible news to share, a miracle," and to hear the happiness in their responses. No more is their response, "I'm so sorry." In its place, the words, "Amazing" "Wonderful." "I'm so thrilled." "You and Jonah must be overjoyed." "Tell me. Tell me what happened. Tell me everything."

And so for the next 18 months, I stand on land at the ocean's edge.

During this period, I enter "outer world life" again—working full-time as a writer, wholeheartedly playing with Jonah and my friends. Raphael and my healing guide, Elizabeth, also encourage me to begin offering "laying-on-of-hands" energy healing for people. During these sessions, I sense Raphael's presence standing behind me, instructing me where to place my hands, "hearing" his guidance for what people can do to unblock any closed-off energy and heal themselves. Many of my clients experience profound emotional, spiritual, and physical shifts and insights.

Every day, I am grateful for this chance at a new beginning. Every day, I am grateful to be able to do again—to live, laugh, love, exert myself, to be of service—without the limitations and encumbrances of illness. And, I'm grateful for the multi-textured growth that has come from the experience of facing illness and abuse—most notably, a heightened compassion for all life and ability to express love and be loved.

Seemingly on course, a renewed sense of purpose and meaning intact, I build what I believe is the new foundation for my life.

But it turns out only to be lovely castles made of sand. After a time, as quickly as I build one, it's slowly washed away with the tide and wind and rain.

Jonah and I take a vacation, traveling through the Southwest. While lazily sitting and relaxing on the bank of a river there, dangling my feet in the seemingly clear, fresh water, splashing it on my arms and face to cool off, I have no idea a new drama is beginning to unfold. From those river waters, I contract the parasite Giardia.

The tide rises higher now.

While I take drugs and herbs to eradicate the Giardia, over the next months, I begin experiencing severe liver pains. I can't eat fat, start losing weight without trying.

Rising faster.

Hepatitis, a gastroenterologist says. We can't figure out how or where I got it. And even though I test negative for Hepatitis A, B, and C, blood work shows my liver levels continue to rise like the tide. "You might have a Hepatitis we don't have a test for," the doctor says. "Or, it still could be C, which might not show up on a test for months."

Potentially life-threatening, he says. But there are options. Interferon. A liver transplant. How reassuring.

And so, I'm in the ocean again. But no longer at one with it. Separate. Afraid.

Turning to face the horizon and the waves, I fall on my knees, eyes closed, hands clasped, praying for guidance, for help from the Divine ones.

The universe's response to me? A sneaker wave rises up, raging and foaming, towering above the other waves, blinding out the sun, the moon, all sources of light. It crashes down on my head, knocks me so down and out with a prizefighter's punch that I don't even see stars or feel my head spin before I lose consciousness. And that rogue wave drags me back out to the open sea. Out and under. Out and under.

On top of everything else that's happened, 18 months after my healing, I have a relapse of CFS.

I sink.

———

In the midst of the relapse, *I dream: I'm living with my father, who's in the background doing yard work. Alan Ginsberg, the poet, appears and asks me, "Do you have any doubt at all that you should be writing a book about incest?"*

"No. I don't," I answer. A fear voice in my head cautions, "It's too much to get into now." I consider admitting that to Alan, but don't, can't, because I know what Alan said is true. This is what I most want, most need to do in my life.

From out of nowhere, an artist appears on the front lawn of my childhood home. She plans to do a massive public painting there. I sense it's linked somehow to the book I'm supposed to write. Propping up a canvas, setting out huge vats of paint, she begins to create.

In real life, however, even though I have thought about writing such a book for several years now, there is no mental concentration, no energy, no will for writing a book on incest or anything else. The dream simply serves as an ache-in-the-heart reminder of that. It reminds me of how much the sexual abuse still impacts my life.

Back in the ocean, scraping the bottom now, I need to focus every ounce of energy I have left to swim up before I drown.

As I relapse, I cut back to doing part-time work from home and stop offering healings. I run to every kind of healer I can think of—a spiritual healer, an acupuncturist who loads me up with Chinese herbs, an MD who gives me IVs of Vitamin C, a chiropractor who has me hold a vile of liquid infused with the energy of Hepatitis, while he does special adjustments on my back that purport to heal the illness. In between, I rest.

But when I do finally swim up to the water's surface, all I can manage are small gulps of air.

My liver levels top out, but remain significantly elevated. I run out of money for alternative treatments. And the self-help processes I learned along the way? They don't seem to work anymore either. Nothing in my healing toolbox helps one little bit.

Barely enough energy to keep my head above water let alone to ride a wave back to shore, the currents pull me out toward the open sea. With the little strength I have, I flail and rage at the ocean, at the Divine, at Raphael, at Elizabeth and Mattie, at the illness, at myself—desperate to make sense of what makes no sense, to find some cause, some order to the dizzying undertow.

But struggling against the ocean gets me nowhere. No land in sight anymore. Eventually, not even any light of day. Only murky darkness. Shadows of ominous creatures swimming around, below me. And still I thrash like a doomed fish caught on a hook and line.

Did I eat too much sugar? Did I not have a good enough attitude? Did I do something? Did I not do something? Could I have done something I didn't?

And I doubt the Divine.

What kind of sadistic Divinity tempts a battered and worn-out fish with the worm-bait of a miraculous healing, lures it with the promised sustenance of succulent, juicy life, only to offer up a life-threatening hook? I use my last ounce of strength, bite the line and sink.

Good-bye, Divine. Good-bye, self esteem. Hello guilt. Hello blame. Hello loss, grief, despair, shame. Yes, shame. Smelly, slimy, fish-innards shame. Shame that somehow, after experiencing a healing, I must face that I'm dealing with no-end-in-sight illness again.

As my heart constricts, I see the possibility before me of hardening into bitterness. But that path I know offers no true relief, would only shut down all that I have worked so hard over the years to open up. It would numb me to myself. So instead, I take the path of what's most alive inside—raw pain.

Seared and bloodied on this journey, I watch my heart break. I watch its shards and slivers fall, each one carrying away a hope, a dream for my life that I lose yet again to illness and to the trauma of abuse that I believe is the illness's cause. I watch, not knowing if anything will ever catch those precious pieces of my heart, or if they will disappear, nosedive endlessly into the pitch-black night.

I hit the bottom of the ocean, stop flailing, and lie still, waiting to drown. I simply let the currents move me this way and that. In the quiet, I hear nothing but my own scattered hope-piercing thoughts. No messages, divine or otherwise. No whale song to lift my heart.

But slowly, slowly, as I wait for water to fill my lungs, spaces appear between the thoughts and rolling currents. I hear my heart beat.

I let the waves of despair wash over me. And while I fear that I have no inner resources left to face this level of illness again, to face more loss of this magnitude, I'm surprised. I *do* survive. The resiliency, resolve, and strength to endure that I gained over the previous six years, added to a lifetime of transcending childhood trauma, remain intact, and in fact, deepen.

In the outer world, I function. I work, see friends, take walks, volunteer at a homeless shelter. Some days and weeks remain deeply messy. Symptoms flare. I hate any healthy person who says, "Things will get better." I want to shred any book that talks about "the gifts" that come from illness and challenges like abuse.

But I know from these last years that a key to enduring is, as much as possible, to live each day, even the messy ones, moment by moment. If I stop to reflect on the past, on what's lost, if I look to the future at what's not possible, or at the potential of living with terminal, or at best chronic, illness, then anger and grief overwhelm me.

Yet when I manage to stay in the present, when I return to the present, I find I can generally cope with whatever happens right in front of my face. When I drop into the moment, I stop pushing the illness away, trying to hold its symptoms at bay. Instead, I love myself, aches and pains and all.

And while I can't live as expansively as I think I'd like to in the outer world, I can and do live expansively and passionately in my inner world. I still travel inward to the deepest recesses of my beingness. And I journey farther than I ever thought possible into other realms and planes of existence.

In those planes, I see that the light of who I am shines ever more brightly as I pass through the darkest of times, and more and more, I bring that wattage of myself back to this reality. It's there, without me having to do or say anything, without me even being conscious of it most times. It's there simply in terms of who I am in the world, in some intangible shining essence of being and accepting and loving and appreciating, which emanates from me when I walk down the street or talk to a friend or a stranger, or simply sit in my house, not even knowing that perhaps I'm illuminating my entire block.

"Do you know what a light you are?" Jonah asks, helping me remember.

"I feel better just being around you," my friend Barbara says. "I don't even know why."

And I understand now that regardless of what my life looks or feels like, I am right on course with a larger purpose for myself, one of knowing and being the divine light within me that exists, regardless of anything that's happened or is happening in my life, of knowing and connecting with the oneness of that light in everyone.

This light of myself is not something I could ever have gained in this world from being the renowned writer I'd hoped to become, or making carloads of money, or measuring up to this world's yardstick of success. Instead, it has come from doing what I'm doing right now, traveling to the underworld stripped of all I know, losing and rediscovering my way on an epic journey—not knowing if I'll live to return to tell the tale. It has been exquisitely honed by pain—from having moments where I tap into the wholeness that exists, that is the truth of me—even now that so much in my life looks and feels broken.

And I learn this about living with debilitating illness and

childhood wounding: Even if my physical condition remains as is, or worsens, no matter how deeply I despair, eventually, I fall into and embrace life *as it is*. I stop pushing my precious life away, even when it's full of suffering. I choose life again and again, as I did in the Babaji dream. This is who I am. This is who I've become on this journey.

And always, always, as I embrace what is, small and large miracles of help and perspective eventually come, often from unexpected places—not only from my loved ones or in meditation, but from the words of a song, a line of dialogue in a movie, some gift from the natural world, or a book I'm drawn to at a bookstore.

Gradually, in this way, the head-on impact of this new bout with illness finds cushioning. All that I've become, all that I've touched of the wholeness inside, recollects it exists. It's larger than what's happening now, and it will go on, continue way beyond this suffering. Even if my body doesn't make it through the testing, this light of myself can't be destroyed. Its essence resonates eternally, a twinkling star often invisible to the naked eye.

Slowly remembering, I ease myself and the Divine off the hook. I forgive myself for getting sick again. I forgive the Divine for allowing it. Neither of us was to blame in the first place. Opening enough to let myself and the Divine back into my wounded, grieving heart, I find a coverlet of fresh, new tissue forming there.

And I don't drown.

Instead, still under water, I breathe.

⌒

In March 1992, 21 months since my father and I last communicated, I receive another letter from him. He writes that despite the fact he was hurt by my accusation and thinks I'm not in my right mind, he agrees to see me. Now, I may be breathing under water when the letter arrives and gaining perspective. But I also remain in a state of heightened vulnerability, easily knocked off my tenuous state of balance. Still, I want this opportunity for the greater healing and forgiveness begun in 1990. From a selfish viewpoint, I hold out hope that a meeting might open me once again to physical healing.

But the letter leaves questions. Is my father willing to talk about the past? How do I really feel now about reconciling with a man who won't admit what he did?

I decide to see him. I want to stand in front of the man who raped me and speak the truth out loud. Perhaps if I speak with an open heart, we will find reconciliation as well. And just as I've accepted my life yet again, even with the illness in it, perhaps I can also take more steps to accept life—even with the abuse in it. I intuit that even greater acceptance than what I've already achieved is a critical next step to my healing. But acceptance isn't about resigning myself to what happened. Rather, it's about having faith that every single event that's occurred was part of a larger plan, even if I don't comprehend how or why. It's incredibly challenging to accept in this way. I know it in my head, but I've yet to live it consistently in my being.

Synchronously, after I finish reading the letter, my mother calls. Over the years since our healing with each other, we're grown even closer. She's been particularly supportive during this latest health emergency. Jonah and I have used up our savings, and even though he is a writer, too, our combined income no longer meets both our living expenses and mounting medical bills. She's been helping us pay medical costs not covered by insurance.

When I tell her about possibly meeting with my father, she cautions me. He only does things for himself, she reminds me, and must have an ulterior motive for writing now. Still, she supports me in whatever I choose to do—see him or not. After we hang up, I wonder if what my mother says is so and what my father's other reason for choosing to see me might be. But the pull toward the possible healing that reconciliation might trigger remains stronger than any concerns her observation brings up in me.

A few days, later, March 31, 1992, a young dove appears on our balcony ledge. It simply sits, trying to hide when it sees

Jonah or me through the sliding glass doors. I wonder whether it fell, or tried to fly, and only got this far. It turns out to be a young dove on its first flight. Throughout the day, its parents come to feed it. They land on the balcony, throats bulging with food, regurgitate it, and stuff it down their baby's beak. I love this new life that has come to visit us.

On that day, I make the decision to see my father. But with conditions. I'll meet only if he's willing to talk about the past, recognizes I'll never "forget" what he did, and accepts that I'll express what I need to whenever I need to. After I write this letter, I set it aside and wait.

Around 4 p.m., the baby dove flies. First, it flies to the roof. I can see its small body and head silhouetted in the shadows on the building next to ours. It calls out the same sounds it made all day to signal its parents. It lifts off and is gone. The dove, symbol of peace, came to our ledge to gather strength for its first flight, and then it flew.

For the next week, the dove phenomenon continues. At least one, sometimes two, young ones come to our balcony every morning and stay until late afternoon. The young doves sit on the ledge or floor, in amidst the driftwood, on the plants. Beautifully and tenderly, a parent lands over and over to feed them. The child is always hungry for more. Then, the young doves take off, ready for solo flight and a new life.

At the week's end, I send the letter to my father. When I don't receive an answer after a few weeks, I call him. Margo picks up. She tells me he decided not to meet with me after all. She's upset because she wanted the two of us to "get over this business." But she won't try to change his mind.

So, my father and I do not meet. But I know I've still done the healing work I was called to do, once more opening my wounded heart in the process.

In late April, I go to a second gastroenterologist, who suggests that Cytomegalovirus, which is common in people with compromised immune systems, may be causing the raised

liver levels rather than hepatitis. Gradually, we move my illness classification back from "life-threatening" to "chronic." By
August, for the first time since December, my liver levels return
to normal and hold firm.

*And so, nine months after submerging, I float up to the ocean's
surface, seaweed woven through my hair, turning my face to the sun.*

October 25, 1992

"Hello, Vita? This is Pat, remember me?"

Pat is Margo's niece, like a second daughter to her. I've
known her since I was 19 years old, when my father met Margo.
Our relationship was one of the casualties of the incest. She
has called me on a Sunday night, seven months after my last
letter to my father. There can be only one likely reason for her
call. Margo or my father is dead or dying. I take a deep breath,
center myself.

"Your father and my aunt asked me to let you know my
aunt has a cancerous brain tumor," she says. "They'd like you
to come as soon as you can."

"I'm so sorry. Of course, I'll come," I say, as if I've been part
of the immediate family all these years. Tears fill my eyes. "Can
you tell me what happened?"

Pat explains that Margo, now 81 years old, started talking in-
coherently, collapsed, and went into convulsions. The doctor on
duty at the hospital said she had a large brain tumor and would
be dead in six weeks. My father had become hysterical, had to
take his "nerve medicine" to calm down. The next day, their personal doctor revised the prognosis, saying she might live from
six months to two years. The brain tumor stemmed from colon
cancer, which had been removed the previous February.

I make a mental note. My father wrote to me right about
that time. Just as my mother had assumed back then, there was
another "reason" for his letter.

I make plans to visit on Wednesday afternoon. Jonah will
accompany me. "I won't pass up what may be my only chance
to see him," I say. "I'm still nervous he might attack me if I

discuss the past, but I won't censor myself—regardless of the circumstances."

"If he makes one move, I'll be all over him," Jonah says. "But I don't think he'd get violent with Margo around."

"You're probably right," I say.

"You're sure you want to put yourself through this?" Jonah asks. "There's no chance he's going to admit what he did."

I sigh. "I confess part of me still hopes for that. In any case, I need to face him and take this opportunity for deeper healing and hopefully, forgiveness. I also want to see Margo. I loved her."

"But she sided with your father," Jonah says.

"That's true," I say. "Listen, I can't say all my motives are pure. I'm sure part of me wants to witness his suffering, too."

"I can understand that," Jonah says.

"Her dying is the worst thing that could happen to him," I say. "He's said his life would be meaningless without her. The way he used to talk, I imagined if she died, he'd go crazy or die from grief. Now, she is dying. If he won't acknowledge the abuse, at least his ordered life has been trashed by this tragedy. Maybe there's some justice in the world after all."

⌒

My father answers the door himself. He has aged some. His face sags a little, his shoulders slump slightly forward, yet he still looks younger than his 76 years—a handsome man in excellent physical shape. Deeply tanned as usual, he combs his silver-gray hair, a little long with pronounced sideburns, swooped up in back in a way that hides the balding on top. Although the outside temperature is barely 60 degrees, he wears shorts and T-shirt, a year-round California uniform that accentuates his muscular build.

He's shorter now, shrunk by aging. We finally stand eye to eye. I relax a bit, feeling more confident Jonah and I can handle him if he loses it.

"Thank God, you've come," he says, tears filling his eyes, as he motions us in. "Jonah. I hoped you'd come, too."

Margo is right behind him smiling, moves forward to take my hands into her own. "My daughter. You're back," she exclaims, slurring her words some, her mouth twisting slightly, as a result of the tumor. "I wanted you back together years ago, but Vally was so hurt"—Vally is the name Margo uses for my father. "I prayed and prayed. Now everything is right again. Thank you for coming."

She has aged more noticeably than my father. She wears a long pink robe and a matching pink turban over her now bald head, her angelic white curls sacrificed to radiation therapy. Her skin is so translucent the veins and capillaries show through on her face. I reach out and hug her tightly, tears flowing from my eyes. Simultaneously, my father hugs Jonah. As soon as I release Margo, my father reaches over and hugs me. I respond stiffly, pull away quickly.

The living room looks like it always has. Jonah and I sit on one of two uncomfortable couches—shellacked wooden frames topped by removable brown, orange and beige patterned foam cushions. My father turns the second couch at a 90-degree angle to ours, so he and Margo can face us more directly. The same old TV/stereo console with an antenna stands against the wall opposite us. The only wall-hanging is a large portrait of my father Margo commissioned for his 60th birthday. Atop an end table are framed photos of Margo's family. One of me used to be there, too, but it's gone. So is the photo of her son-in-law who died from cancer a year earlier.

Arms gesticulating, my father launches into talking about how Margo's illness has impacted his nerves, how his anti-depressant medication no longer works. He doesn't mention Margo's condition until I ask. I find out that in addition to radiation, they're going to the fundamentalist Christian church they attend for a laying on of hands healing. They're hoping for a miracle.

"You know, I have healing energy in my hands, too," my father announces. "It may not be strong enough to heal someone, like our minister can, but when I put my hands on Margo's head, she feels energy, and her pain goes away."

He tells me that his own mother was a healer, too. People from the neighborhood came to her for healings. I am shocked. I know my father is quite psychic, a trait he and I share. I know his mother taught him how to read prescient symbols in life and in dreams. But I never knew about this shared family healing trait.

The healer I knew in my family was my maternal grandmother, who used herbs to heal her family, friends, and neighbors. I thought the laying on of hands healing ability I'd opened to in myself and utilized for others during my temporary healing from CFS had been passed on to me from her.

How could the man who raped me have healing ability? When I tell him about my own experiences, he exclaims, "Oh my God. You really are like me."

I cringe inside. "I don't do it anymore because I had a relapse of the illness." This is the first time they learn I'm still dealing with CFS.

"Maybe some day I will lay my hands on you," my father says to me. "Wouldn't it be funny if I could help you get better?"

Every muscle in my body clenches. Funny is not exactly the word I have in mind when thinking about him laying his hands on me. *Not in this lifetime*, I think. *I don't care how much I forgive you.*

We continue to talk like we're simply catching up on each other's lives, when my father says, "It's so good we're a family again after the years we lost—over nothing."

Blood pounds in my temples. *Nothing?* I instantly move out of the cancer drama to the other drama being played out here. "The years weren't lost for nothing. There's a very real reason why I haven't been here. And when you say we're family again, I'm still not sure. All I know for sure now is that I'll be talking to you about the past anytime feelings come up concerning it—regardless of whether or not we agree on what that past is."

"Of course," he says quickly.

I'm stunned. *This is too easy*, I think. *He must not have heard me. But I let the thought slide.*

My father wants to know about the apartment I live in. Jonah and I have moved to a one-bedroom apartment in West Los Angeles. As I speak, he brings out a pad and pencil. "I want you to tell me exactly how to get there," he says, holding them out toward me. "Draw a map. We can visit you."

"Hold on, Papa," I answer. "This is too fast for me."

He backs off. "Of course. I understand. Tell me when it feels right."

About the time I wonder if he and I will ever get a chance to talk alone, he offers us tea and cookies. When I tell them I don't eat refined sugar or drink coffee now because of the illness, he gets upset because he doesn't have a snack for me.

"Water's fine," I say. He shakes his head, blurts out excitedly, "Grapes! What about grapes? Can you eat them?"

"Yes, that would be nice," I respond.

He laughs out loud, his hand slapping his knee. "Grapes. I forgot we had them. They don't set right with my stomach. But, yesterday, on a whim, I thought, 'I'm going to buy grapes to see if I can eat them again.' Now I have them for you. I'm so happy. Isn't it amazing? Come into the kitchen to show me how many you want."

This is it. As close an opportunity as I'm going to get to talk alone with him. So, as my father stands at the sink washing a handful of grapes, I ask, "What did you expect would happen when you had Pat call me?"

Looking surprised, his mouth falls open slightly. He averts his eyes from direct contact. "Well, that we'd forget the past and be a family again." Today, my father speaks to me in accented English, instead of Latvian, and I respond in kind.

"Listen, despite what's happened, I want for us to heal, too," I say, with an even tone. "But I can never forget the past. When feelings come up for me about sexual or physical abuse, I must be free to talk about them," repeating what I don't think he heard earlier.

"Of course," he says as quickly as he did before, looking straight at me now. "We'll talk right away and clear it up."

"You know, too, that our views on the past differ," I say. "I remember sexual abuse. You deny it. You think something's wrong with my memory. I think you won't admit it, or you've blocked it out. But I still need to talk about the past if we continue meeting."

"Fine," he says, putting the grapes in a bowl. Then, he launches into his version of events, repeating he only beat me three times. I interrupt, "I remember much more, and so does Mamma," and proceed to reiterate the regular abuse.

"Well, maybe I did do that," he says. "I don't know. I'd get so mad at your mother, or at my life, that I'd see red. I wouldn't remember what I did." He avoids my eyes again. "I only hit you when you were bad. But you were also very obedient. I remember once you had a tantrum. I hit you and you never had one again."

"I stopped, because I didn't feel free to express anything," I say. "I was scared, not obedient. I lived in fear of you every day of my childhood. I was afraid to laugh out loud or move suddenly. I never knew when you'd lose your temper."

He reaches over and pulls me to him, hugs me. "But how could you be afraid of me? I loved you so much."

"I never felt it," I say, gently, while firmly pulling back from his hug. "You didn't express it. What you expressed was anger and criticism. I thought you hated me."

"But all this is in the past," he says in a pleading tone. He starts crying.

I feel a tug on my energy, like he's sucking energy from my eyes through his own eyes and voice. When I look at him, I notice his face remains mobile. Yet his eyes have a deadness, a rigidity. I take a deep breath and imagine roots growing out my feet into the earth to ground myself. I close my eyes, breaking contact, and imagine an extra layer of protective light around me. I call back my energy, feel it return.

"I'm a changed man," he says, passionately, emotion oozing toward me. He reaches his hand to cover my own, which rests on the counter. "I haven't hit anybody in years."

"You may be changed." I draw my hand out from under his, let it rest along my side. "But I'm dealing with the scars left by the man you were. I have feelings from that past I couldn't deal with then. So I'm dealing with them now."

"I understand," he says and abruptly stops crying. "Let's deal with them."

Who is this man? I ask myself. The father I knew would never talk this much about these issues. He'd tell me to get out of his house and life.

In the few times we had discussed the past, even when he would stick around to listen, instead of taking responsibility, he'd quickly flick away what I said as easily as if it were a fly landing on his arm. His favorite "flick" was blaming others. He couldn't help his violent temper, because my mother didn't love him enough. He yelled when I was a teenager, because he was jealous I spent my free time with my boyfriend. I'd felt confused the first time I heard my father say he was jealous, but the jealousy took on new meaning when I remembered the incest.

Now, on the surface, talking about the past does seem different this time. Even if he still isn't taking much responsibility, he's staying with the subject. I'm still not sure, though. While important, this entire dialogue is secondary, because what I most want is to talk about incest. What I most want is for him to scream, "Yes, I sexually abused you." Then, I want him to fall at my feet, and confess, "I'm so ashamed. I'm totally wrong. I beg your forgiveness. I can never make up for it, but I'm dedicating the rest of my life to trying."

I look again into my father's dead eyes, hoping they will reveal to me he knows he is culpable. In the background, I hear Jonah and Margo talking. They laugh from time to time, Jonah's voice a soft reassurance.

"Let's get through this, so we can move on," my father says. "We've already lost years of our lives together—over nothing. Let's not lose more time."

"Nothing?" I say again, controlling my emotions, heart pounding. I continue to look right into those eyes. "I wouldn't call sexual abuse *nothing*. That tore me apart and affected every area of my life, including my health. To say it still hurts doesn't begin to touch the depth of what I feel. It's not nothing. Stop saying that."

"Okay, okay. I don't want to start anything. I know what you think," he says, putting his hands in front of him in a stopping motion. "Listen, we were naked together when you were little. We'd be in the shower. Maybe that's what you're confusing."

"There's no confusion on my part. What I remember goes way beyond being naked," I cut him off, my voice excited, but not raised. I've still never yelled at my father in person, only at "pillow representations" of him in therapy.

Gradually, though, as I voice the words about incest, I'm surprised to note the fear I had that he would physically harm me if I spoke the truth at any volume level begins to crumble. It's turned to ash by a fire rising inside me. What emerges is a picture of a woman ready to do whatever is necessary to protect herself and those she loves against the man who would rape or otherwise violate them.

Voldemars lowers his eyes, talks in that pleading, energy-sucking voice again. "That time you accused me was so hard," he says. "I was upset for two weeks."

"*Two weeks?*" I say, agitated. "I've suffered for *years*. If that's all you suffered, you're way ahead of the game. But I'm really tired of hearing how sad I made you. How this affects you. Not once have I heard you say how sad you are you hurt *me*. Not for the incest. Not for hitting me. Not for your screaming fits and constant criticism. I hurt, Papa. I'm in pain. You're not my victim here. I'd like you to acknowledge *my* pain for once."

Silence. Five seconds. Ten. Twenty. Again, he looks at me with eyes that tug on my energy. *Weird*, I think. I've become so much more sensitive to how energy feeds and drains me, to how it moves or gets blocked in my body as a result of the illness. Once more, I pull my energy back. Yet at the same time, I persist in searching for a sign that gives him away, that tells me for certain he's conscious of having molested me.

And finally, I get it. Not as I expect by a look in his face, but in the shadow that enshrouds him like the head of a King Cobra. It reveals itself, expanding and receding. A dark, creeping, toxic energy with a deadly bite. A shudder ricochets through my body. In this silent revelation, my gut tells me what his words don't—that he remembers. He knows exactly what he did. It's all there in front of me. He doesn't have to say a word.

Seeing how fully the cobra energy grips him, I probably should have left his house right then and never returned, but I don't. I tell myself that now that I know it is present, I can dodge its fangs. I believe that as long as I remain mindful, I won't be harmed. Besides, I still think I need to be here in order to heal the abuse fully in my body and spirit. So I stay.

Voldemars finally speaks. "Well, I did feel bad when I hit you. But I wasn't able to talk to your mother or to you about that—or about what I was going through. It was hard adjusting to this country and working in a job I hated. But you kept quiet, too. You never told me how you felt."

"I was a little child," I say. "You were the adult. There was no way to talk to you, even if I'd known what to say. I tried to stay out of your way."

"I understand," he says, and reaches over to hug me. I don't hug back. "Remember, Vita. We're flesh and blood. Nothing can change that. I loved you from the day you were born, and even while we've been apart. You have no idea how often I picked up a pen to write you a letter. But I stopped, because I was too scared. I prayed each week at church to give me my daughter back. Now I know God works in strange ways. He had to give me this tragedy so that I could heal with you and Margo's daughter, Sandy. She's scared of me, too. So, that's that." He lets go of me and moves back. "If anything comes up about the past, we'll peacefully resolve it."

"I can't promise that," I say. "I'm willing to try to heal, but our conversations may not be peaceful. I may get angry. And I don't know that we'll resolve anything. Without your admitting what you did, I *don't* feel resolved right now."

"Okay. Okay. Whatever you need to do," he says.

I look at this man, bewildered. His conceding even this much amazes me. I'm not used to him expressing this much love or cooperation. With a dramatic gesture, and a determined look,

Voldemars points toward a hanging calendar with cat photos tacked to the wall. "What's today's date?" he asks, running his finger across the days. "October 28th. That's it. Every year, we'll celebrate our own special holiday, the day we became father and daughter again."

As we return to the living room, with the coffee, tea, grapes, and cookies, he repeats how great it is we're a family again. This time, I don't stop him.

"My daughter," Margo says, slurring the words, reaching over to touch my hand when I sit down. "I've got my daughter back."

Margo and I are both noticeably tired. So after we have our refreshments, we say our good-byes. Everyone hugs, and my father tells Jonah he is family, too.

"So we'll see each other again," I say, as we walk out the door. "Soon," Margo and my father echo, as if this is a normal parting of a daughter with her father and stepmother.

"Tell me what you thought first," I ask Jonah, as we drive out of their residential area filled with brick and wood ranch houses similar to my father's. Many have children's bikes and toys scattered in the yards.

"When I look at your father, I see a tortured man," Jonah says. "On the one hand, he's totally cut off from himself. On the other, he's so emotional, so open and raw. I've only met him three times, but his vulnerability is right out there. I'm shocked, actually. I've never met a man like that. I couldn't believe the warmth he kept pouring at us."

I listen, propping my head up against the glass pane, tired but adrenaline-charged.

"I'm also surprised at my reaction," Jonah says. "I expected to want to bash him for what he's done, to hate him even more seeing him in person. Instead, I found myself feeling compassion for what distortion has come out of him. Your conversation in the kitchen blew my mind. I didn't hear all of it. But I couldn't believe your father took what I did hear without blowing up.

Half of me was having this pleasant conversation with Margo, who's so charming and intelligent. The other half of me listened to you, thinking, 'Here we go.' I knew exactly where our things were, so I could snatch them as we ran out the door. Ultimately, the visit seemed like a miracle."

"Maybe you're right," I answer, hoping he is. "It does seem incredible. But this is my father, the master manipulator. I'd trust what took place more if Margo wasn't terminally ill. He must be terrified of losing her and being alone. I'm his only family. I don't know if anyone in her family even feels close enough to continue seeing him after she dies."

"So that might be the only reason he took so much from you," Jonah says.

"It might be," I say. "But I'm really happy I saw Margo. I'm thrilled I had the chance to physically face my perpetrator and live through it. There seemed to be an opening. We still have a long way to go. But my impulse is to go for all the healing I can."

"Maybe your father has actually changed," Jonah says. "Maybe he feels guilty about the past and wants to fix it the best he can without admitting it. I can't imagine how he lives knowing he molested you. I'm sure he remembers. That's my gut feeling when I look at him. Don't you think?"

I relate the cobra experience.

"I trust that," Jonah comments. "It's believable. Anyone who meets him for long has to see he's twisted."

"That's true. But how can someone who's that twisted, who has committed abuse like he has, have laying on of hands healing ability?" I ask. "It's too weird that he and I share that—and that he mentioned it. He's never talked to me about it before—or his mother's healing ability."

"Well, I admit it's strange, but if you think about it spiritually, it makes sense," says Jonah. "If you believe like I do—and I know you do—that every person has the Divine within them, then every person also has the potential to act from that divine consciousness—even abusers, like your father, and even if it's only for a moment and their divine light is very small. He must tap into that inner divinity when he does healing."

At home, I sleep for 12 hours straight, wake up more energized than I've been since the relapse. My mind is clear. My muscles and joints are pain-free.

Later, when I meditate, I open my heart further to compassion for my father and myself. For the first time in a very long while, I sense the Archangel Raphael with me, my beloved healing angel. He showers me with shooting stars of light that fill every cell of my being with Divine Love. Just like I experienced the first time he appeared to me, afterward, I find that I have more vitality and fewer CFS symptoms—a definite improvement in physical well-being.

Once more, I believe I'm experiencing firsthand the healing power of love and forgiveness, a strong motivator to keep on reconciling with my father. But I also am under the belief, misguided as it will turn out to be, that for this healing to complete itself, I will need to continue meeting with him—even if he doesn't admit what he did. Over the coming weeks, I pay a high price for this belief.

That evening, I tell my mother about meeting with my father. She pauses, then says, "I support what you need to do to heal. If that includes seeing your father, then do that. But remember Valdis' wife is dying. Maybe the reason he called you now isn't because he loves you and wants to heal. Maybe he just wants somebody to take care of him."

"That certainly crossed my mind as a possibility," I say, disappointed.

"Take care of yourself," she says. "And don't let the tragedy in their lives drain you. Don't sacrifice your health to take care of them. I love you and don't want you hurt by this man any more than you already have been."

"He did seem to be more open," I say.

"Be careful," she says. "Over the years, nothing I've heard about your father has led me to believe he's different. His old friends have told me when they visit him in San Diego, everything centers only around what he wants to do. Even *they* comment on his narcissism. Voldemars is out for number one. Always has been, always will be."

"You're right, Mamma; I can't argue with what you're saying," I reply, but silently I resist it anyway. "At the same time, I've got to do this. "

"God keep you safe then," she says.

———

Song of Life

Jonah and I take advantage of the fact that I'm feeling better by traveling to Joshua Tree National Monument, near Palm Springs, to celebrate. Joshua Tree is a powerful expanse of high desert that looks like God threw down piles upon piles of huge boulders and balanced them in impossible ways.

The Joshua trees, which highlight the park, are a form of yucca tree. Known as survivor trees, they first shoot out one stalk as a branch. When that branch is damaged by weather or wildlife, a new shoot grows right below the damaged shoot, continuing the life of the tree. The process repeats again and again. The result is short, gnarly, cactus-like trees, strange beings with grass skirts and odd-looking branches that curve up, reaching to the sky.

Late one afternoon, we hike amongst the Joshua trees and rock piles to an isolated spot with an expansive view. We're the only people in sight. I find a piece of white opaque quartz crystal shaped like a horse's head. This is significant to me because early in the illness journey, an image of a white horse came to me, a symbol of my creativity. I received a message then to call forth the energy of the horse to help me whenever I wanted to write. For months back then, I envisioned myself riding the white horse naked, without bridle, saddle, or reins. I somehow knew that if I could ride this way with total love and faith, the horse, and the creativity it inspired, would take me anywhere I wanted to go. It would bring the unlimited into the limited that was my present existence.

I still keep a statue of a white horse on my desk at home and photos and drawings of white horses on the wall. Now, I have a new white horse symbol to represent a heightened level of creative healing.

Holding the rock, I'm inspired to strip, to stand naked in the desert, like I've imagined myself riding naked on the white horse. I tell Jonah, and he wants to join me. Giggling like two kids getting away with something naughty, the two of us peel away layers of clothing. Arms outstretched to the heavens, we stand naked in the silence, feel the cool fall air against our bodies. I sing a song that a healer suggested a couple of years earlier as part of my healing. "Sing your name," the healer told me. "Vita. Sing, 'I am Vita.' Breathe it in, and think of what it means: *Life*." My name, she explained, was already a healed state with which I could identify. It replaced the helplessness from childhood wounding and the illness with "I am Vita, a being of life and light and energy."

She continued, "Stay with this song with the persistence of a Himalayan monk chanting mantras, spinning the prayer wheel, living the sparse life in order to know God. It will help clear your past and heal your body to be able to move forward with the mission that God has intended for you."

Afterward, I sang every day for a couple of months. I sang in our apartment. I sang in the car. I sang strolling around the block. I made up melodies that came out like classical choral pieces—my own spontaneous Handel's *Messiah*, celebrations of my life and spirit. "I am Vita. I am Life. I am energy and vitality. I am heal–ed and inspir–ed. I am Vita. I am Life." Back then, I sang even when all my symptoms were flared up. Sometimes, Jonah sang along with me. We played with the melodies and laughed together. That was during the period I started to experience a gradual improvement of the CFS. I had the first healing experience with Raphael. I felt lighter and more hopeful. After the healing, I stopped singing.

But now, here in Joshua Tree, I sing again, "I am Vita. I am life," and Jonah sings with me. Our audience is the Joshua trees. They look like they're waving at us. Cheering us on, these compatriot survivors acknowledge two more survivors of damage standing in their midst, ever reaching to the sky.

When we finish, Jonah, who loves the *Wizard of Oz*, says, "Toto, I don't think we're in Kansas anymore." I laugh. We are definitely out of the tornado and in Oz. I may still have to ride the white horse to Emerald City. With my human and spirit helpers, I may have to face the Wicked Witch. But I am deeply grateful for the infusions of grace and life force that have appeared to assist me on the Yellow Brick Road.

———

A small light in the dark room highlights Margo's unconscious face and white-turbaned head. She sleeps on her side, curled in a fetal position, clutching her blanket to her chest, breathing heavily. The first doctor was right. Six weeks after her first attack, Margo is back in the hospital, this time in a coma. Her tumor has enlarged. She might not last the day.

Trusting that people in comas can hear what's said to them, I've been sitting next to her saying my good-byes. I've come alone this time—Jonah has a writing deadline—and plan to stay for a few days. A hand gently touches my shoulder. It's Pat, Margo's niece. She looks like she did the last time I saw her seven years earlier—attractive, short, frosted-blond hair, slim. She's 42 now, wears tight jeans and a casual blue sweater. She and my father were off at dinner when I arrived an hour before this.

I feel awkward. It's the first time I've seen Pat since I remembered the incest. Do I hug her? Shake her hand? I opt for the hug, and she responds warmly. I'm grateful.

"I'm glad you're here," she says. "I don't know if I could handle this alone." She tells me my father cried for two hours non-stop that morning and that his antidepressant medicine isn't working. The doctor has set up an appointment with a psychiatrist, because the case is beyond his skill as an internist. Before she can say anymore, my father comes into the room and gives me a big hug. He looks at Margo, shrugs his shoulders, goes to sit in the furthest corner from her. "I can't look at her," he says. "Every time I look, I cry. And I can't cry."

"It's okay," I say. "It's normal to cry when your wife is dying."

"No. I've got to stay strong," he says, closing his eyes and shaking his head back and forth. "Once I start, I can't stop. My sweet Margo's gone."

"I'm so sorry, Papa. I know this is hard," I say. "But she's not gone yet. People can hear what you say to them while they're unconscious. Tell her anything. She'll know."

"Yes, I've heard that, but it's too painful," he says. "It's better if I'm over here."

At that moment, the doctor arrives and gives the latest update on Margo's condition. She might die quickly or linger in and out of a coma for a few weeks. In a couple of days, she won't need a hospital anymore. He suggests a hospice. We plan to visit one the next morning.

After he leaves, Pat tells my father she'd like to introduce me to the nurses. But when we get outside the room, she motions me aside. "I didn't get to tell you. Earlier today, the doctor told me your father has a panic disorder and will be on medication the rest of his life. Hopefully, the psychiatrist can figure out what kind will help—and maybe give him counseling."

"Panic disorder," I say to myself, mixed emotions welling inside. On the one hand, I'm sorry. On the other, I'm not sure what this means. I'm definitely not ready to be a caregiver for the man who molested me. I also wonder if this will be one more excuse for my father not to discuss the past. Panic disorder, dying wife or not. I need to honor my own feelings by discussing issues as they arise and do what's most healing and loving for me—or I can't be here.

Back at the house that evening, Pat also tells me that Margo, who handled the finances, had let the bills slide. She points to an overflowing pile of papers and envelopes, many unopened. Some are overdue notices and collection threats. Judy, my father's neighbor and close friend, has offered to help. Pat asks if I want to handle my father's bills instead. I decline, then after a short conversation about our lives, I excuse myself and go to my room to unpack.

My father comes in. My throat and chest constrict at being alone in a small bedroom with him. I breathe deeply and remind myself that Pat is right in the next room. He starts talking about coming to stay with me in Los Angeles on weekends, maybe selling his house and moving there—to be near me. *No way*, I scream inside. *Mistake. I can't do this. Mistake.* Outwardly, I calmly list reasons why that won't work.

After my father goes to bed, exhausted, I stop unpacking, put on a nightgown, and climb into bed to read and try to relax. Ten minutes later, there's a knock. In walks my father, dressed in a bright red v-neck nightshirt that stops mid-thigh. He clutches his chest, looks panicky. "I need your help," he says, grabbing my arm, pulling me with him. "Please, you've got to come. You've got to put your hands on me like I do for my Margo. Come on my bed and put your hands on me."

Adrenaline shoots through my body. I'm a seven-year-old child again. Is he really saying what I hear? He wants me to come in his bedroom and touch him. I am ready to scream for Pat. Is he losing control, revealing he molested me by asking me to participate again? Blood drums in my ears; my chest and face are red hot.

"Like I put my hands on Margo's head, and you do for people, too," he runs on. "My chest is so tight. I can't breathe. I want you to give me a healing until I fall asleep."

A healing, I repeat to myself and the seven-year-old inside me, as rationally as I can. Not molestation. A healing. I still can't believe he'd ask this of me.

"I c-ca-an't," I stutter, the words stumbling through the pounding in my throat. I automatically pull the blanket up to my chin, sit up straight, as if doing so offers me protection. "I'm not doing healings anymore, remember? Because of the illness?"

My voice begins to calm down. "Take some deep breaths, Papa. Like this." I inhale deeply, showing him how to breathe all the way down to his navel and exhale all the way out again. "You'll be okay. Your sleep medicine will kick in soon."

Looking like a young child, he listens, mimics me, breathing in and out. "Whoa, that is better," he says. "Thank you. I understand. You have to take care of yourself. I understand. I feel better. I really do."

"It's been a long day, Papa," I say, my seven-year-old needing him out of the room. "I'm tired. Let's try to get some sleep."

"Okay. I'll go back to my room," he says. "Deep breathing. You know, my doctor told me about that. I keep forgetting. It's good. It's good." He closes my door.

Hypervigilant, mind racing, I am wide awake now, completely triggered. I take a Chinese herb I've brought along to help me sleep. But at 3:30 a.m., I still can't sleep. Rational or not, I'm afraid to fall asleep in my father's house. The few times I start to nod off, I jerk awake. I finally realize that being here, staying even for a few days is much too much for me. Panic attacks. Financial problems. Dying wife. My father wanting to come to LA. The feelings—his and my own—are too overwhelming.

Time to backtrack. I thought I could just be here and witness, experience that I could survive being with my father on my own. But that's impossible. My natural tendency is also to help someone in pain. But this is not a natural situation. And I refuse to take care of my father. I need to be back home. Off the front lines, where I can deal with my conflicted feelings on my own. I decide to return to LA the following evening.

At 6:30 a.m., as soon as I hear my father up, I go into the kitchen. He's making himself the same breakfast he has since I was a child—a sandwich—half goose liver and half cream cheese and butter. Back then, I used to get grossed out that anyone could eat goose liver. He has also put out his standard bowl of instant oatmeal. Orange juice. A cup of instant coffee with non-dairy creamer and one spoonful of sugar. When I was a teenager, he added a special energy health-food drink—a large breakfast to prepare for hard labor at the steel mill. At

76, he continues to do heavy yard work and swim a mile every morning.

"You're up early. Did you sleep all right?" my father asks. "After you told me about that deep breathing, I went right to sleep. Here, I'm putting instant oatmeal in a bowl for you. Do you still eat it?

"Yes," I say. "But I can fix my own breakfast later. Why don't you sit down and eat? I want to talk."

He looks at me like a puppy that's been slapped with a newspaper. "Vita . . .don't. . .I can't. . .talk about that."

"I'm not asking you to speak directly about that," I say. "I just didn't sleep at all. Being here is bringing up difficult feelings from the past for me. I understand you can't deal with that right now. At the same time, I'm concerned about my own health."

"Black. . .black. . .I'm seeing black. . .m-my pills. My nerve pills—" My father starts gasping and choking, pointing to pills in a bottle. I bring them with a glass of water.

"I can't," he says. "I can't talk about the past. My wife is dying. My Margo." He puts one hand on his heart, extends the other toward me as if to ward off physical attack.

"Listen, Papa. I'm not expecting you to," I say. "I know you're handling all you can. At the same time, I can't control my feelings. And, frankly, I don't want to. I've stuffed them down too long So, it's best for me that I leave. I'll stay for the day, then drive home this evening."

"But can we still be father and daughter?" he asks, the panic gone in an instant.

"Yes," I say.

"And. . .I can come visit?" he asks.

"It would be better if you come for the day only," I say.

"Yes, for the day," he says. "I can drive up in the morning, and we can take a walk together. I'll walk behind you and Jonah. I won't get in the way. I promise. Or, I'll sit quietly and watch while you work. You're right. I want you to stay, but I don't want you to get sicker."

"We'll work something out," I say. "I know this is hard for

you. But it's hard for me, too, not being able to talk to you."

"I can't, Vita. . .please. . .don't," he says, cowering, as if I'm hitting him.

"It's okay," I say. "That's all I've got to say."

My father, Pat, and I sit huddled in the far corner of Margo's hospital room. The curtains are drawn back; sunlight streams in. A nurse sits by Margo's bedside to make sure Margo doesn't hurt herself. Sometimes, she thrashes out of control or goes into convulsions.

The more time I spend with my father, the more confused and ambivalent I feel. On the one hand, my father continues to surprise me like he did during my first post–incest discussion. On our hospice tour earlier in the day, he told the administrator that Margo made his life heaven on earth. He agreed to do grief counseling—and to spend nights in Margo's hospice room with her until she dies. He liked my suggestions to bring family photos from home and flowers from their garden to brighten up what will be her room there. When I hear him talk like this, I have hope that in the future, he and I can discuss the abuse again and find more healing.

But now back in the hospital room, he's once more calling himself a baby for crying. He doesn't want to sit at Margo's bedside or talk to her, even if she can understand him. He and Pat both agree Margo is already gone, and my father is the one who needs help, not Margo.

Old anger about his narcissism resurfaces inside me like a smoldering cigarette butt thrown into a dry summer forest waiting to burst. But I keep extinguishing its embers, telling myself my father and Pat have a right to do what they want. I'm the outsider here. They're the true family.

"Margo has left me. I have to think of myself," my father says. "In fact, I'm not even coming to the hospital in the mornings anymore. I'm going back to my schedule of swimming every day, starting now. I'm a survivor. I'll start a new life. Only, I'm not sure how."

"There are senior centers in your area," I say.

"Yes. That's good. Maybe I'll go to a senior center and meet another woman," he says. And as Margo lies nearby dying, we're suddenly having a conversation about my father finding a new relationship. I feel queasy, uncomfortable participating, but I do.

He changes the subject, tells us he and Margo want to be cremated and have their ashes scattered in the Pacific Ocean from a plane. But he'll have someone from the cremation service go up for him and scatter hers. He doesn't want to do it himself. "Margo will understand. She already told me. No funeral. No eulogy. She knows I couldn't take it. Even when she had this last seizure, I lost control. I smashed my fist into the wall and started pulling at my hair. I wanted to yank it out of my head."

But I don't understand why he won't go up in the plane. I feel more and more critical, judgmental. When my father talks about losing control, I feel anxious. It's too reminiscent of my childhood. Yet I say nothing. *It's not my way, but I need to honor theirs*, I repeat to myself.

Without any warning, my father stands up, goes to Margo's bedside. He takes off his shirt and T-shirt, and before we know it, he stands in the room, his still well-toned, muscular chest bare. Margo's nurse gapes at him and jumps up, startled.

"I'm getting into bed with my wife," he says to her, laughing.

"Would you like me to give you some privacy?" she asks, bewildered, looking from me to Pat. We're as confused as she is. I shrug my shoulders at her, look at my father, say awkwardly, "Papa, we'll all leave if you want some time alone with Margo."

He laughs out loud now. "I'm kidding. I got hot, that's all. I wanted to take off my undershirt. It's hot in here. Please sit." He motions to the nurse. "You don't have to go away. I'm just an old man trying to cool off."

The nurse, her eyes wide, laughs, too, albeit nervously. "Oh. I didn't know. . . No one's ever done anything like that. . . Then I thought, why not? It's your wife."

My father, shrugs sheepishly, puts his shirt back on, folds the undershirt neatly, and returns to our corner territory.

⌒

That evening, I drive home, speeding all the way, grateful to have Jonah's arms waiting to envelop me. Shaking with exhaustion, pushed way beyond my CFS limits, I shower anyway, scrubbing hard with a loofah brush to remove the smell of the hospital. The next day, I sleep until noon, awakening to a full flaring of CFS symptoms. The day after, I come down with a cold.

⌒

My father calls nightly now, each time in a panic. When he sees the psychiatrist, my father tells her he doesn't want counseling. All he wants are pills to take away the pain. None of them work. I feel like a toxic waste dump for my father's never-ending pain and need. Yet, telling him to stop calling while his wife is dying feels cruel. So I listen. I look for homeopathic remedies to help him with the panic. I call senior centers and have them mail him brochures. I realize I'm being a caregiver, like I said I wouldn't be, but rationalize this is the bare minimum I'd do for anyone I know in pain.

During this time, he drastically cuts the time he spends visiting Margo, who is now at the hospice. He puts only his photo on her bedside table—no one else's. Instead of spending nights there like he said he would, he visits only an hour or two a day. "Too much like sleeping with a dead person," he says. "I've gone back to my routine—swimming, working out, doing yard work."

Anger wells up in me. No longer old anger gnawing at me from the past, but fresh, new anger. *This is how he lets the woman who created "heaven on earth" for him die. Alone.* But I contain my rage, and repeat in the controlled voice that has cost me dearly over the years, "Even if she's in a coma, she needs you now, too."

"She's gone," he cuts in. "Oh, the nurses tell me she comes in and out of consciousness, but I can't wait for those times. Yesterday, they even had her sitting up in a chair. I sat next to her, and she held my hand so tightly. She couldn't talk, but I could tell she understood me. I left while she sat there."

I knew my father was narcissistic. But I never believed he was capable of deserting Margo during this sacred transition. I thought he'd be by her side every minute.

"And that grief therapy," he runs on without stopping for a breath. "I went to one session, and the therapist asked, 'How are you feeling?' Can you imagine? I thought therapy was like a pep talk where he'd tell me, 'Everything's going to be okay.' I'm never going back."

So in that moment, since my father can't let himself be sad, I am instead. For him. For Margo. But most of all for myself. Sad at how impossible this situation has become for me. His distortion, his pathology, his narcissism are all finally too much to bear. Any thoughts I might enjoy witnessing his suffering are long gone. I don't enjoy it, and I don't like my own either. I am buffeted by conflicting feelings. The love and forgiveness I felt before ever visiting, the power and promise of our first meeting, have now been joined and polluted by anger, judgmentalness, confusion, mistrust, and fear. Instead of experiencing healing, I feel worse emotionally and physically.

As I lose my grounding, I "should" myself. *I shouldn't feel so negative toward him when he's going through this tragedy. I should be understanding, compassionate. I should still feel forgiving.* If I don't, am I any better than the man I'm judging?

I also cling to the remotest possibility he'll be so desperate to keep me in his life, he might admit what he did. I hope I can keep my mouth shut until we can discuss the past again, but I'm a mess. The emotional distance and centeredness I maintained during our first meeting is long gone. I only sleep a couple of hours a night. So, as my father reduces the time he spends with Margo, I reduce the time I spend with him, telling him to call only every other day. "I already have a cold," I say. "I'm sorry you're hurting, but every time we talk, I need the whole day to recover, and the next day, you call again."

Less than one week after Margo's arrival at the hospice, and 10 days after she went into a coma, my father announces he's no longer even going to visit for an hour a day. In fact, the next day, he's not going to see her at all.

~~~~~~~

The very day my father first stays away, a few minutes after 11 a.m., at the time he would have been visiting, Margo dies. It is December 16th, my own mother's birthday.

Jonah and I drive down on Saturday to see him for the day. When I walk into the house, Margo's family is there, too. Pat sits at the desk doing paperwork. Margo's daughter, Sandy, is resting in a bedroom.

"Jonah. . .Vita. . .Thank God, you're here," my father says, hugging us each separately, then both at once, pulling us into the living room. "I'm doing okay, but I was a bad boy this morning. I started going through Margo's things and read part of a love letter she wrote to me. I started to cry."

"It's okay, Papa," I say. "She died only two days ago."

"No, no. It's not okay for my nerves," he says. "I don't want to talk about her, and I don't want anyone else to talk about her."

"Not even today?" I ask, incredulously.

"Yes," he says.

All afternoon, we sit in the living room with the family making small talk, forbidden by my father to mention Margo's death—or her life.

We're also ignoring another elephant in the room. Pat and Sandy are the very same people who chose over these years to believe my father rather than me, when he denied the incest—and of course I can't discuss that subject under these circumstances either. *How could they believe this clearly disturbed man over me?* I wonder as I watch them talking to one another. There are long uncomfortable pauses in the conversations. My chest tightens each time I stop myself from discussing Margo or the incest. Jonah holds my hand, squeezes it often. I keep repeating to myself, *I can leave anytime I want; and in my own home, I can express any feeling I want.*

After dinner, the conversation dwindling down to what movies we want to see over the holidays, Jonah and I prepare to leave. My father motions us aside. "You and Jonah are my Guardian Angels," he says in a hushed voice. We stand huddled together, away from the others. He puts an arm around each of us. "You're so calm, so helpful.".

Calm, my ass. I'm about as calm as a hurricane. Angelic? My thoughts and feelings are anything but. A scream mounts inside.

"Anyway, I love you both. Thanks for being here," he says.

As he speaks, I once again experience the tug on my energy I felt during our first meeting. This time though, emotionally wrung out, I can't release myself.

"I'll be all right," he says. "Things may be rough for a while, but I'll find another woman. Not as good as Margo, but someone."

My father hugs me, and I walk out the door. *Stay out of fear and anger*, I hear in my head. *They are what give him power over you.* Wise advice from a wise part of me. But in this moment, I'm fresh out of forgiveness, tolerance, and balance, and fresh into new depths of anger. I don't like this feeling, don't like who I am with him during this time of loss. Not a guardian angel. Not even a loving human, but a judge, sentencing not only my father, but also myself.

In the car, Jonah immediately says, "I knew your father was crazy, but that was the weirdest wake I've ever been to. It was like we were pretending Margo never existed."

"Surreal," I say, oblivious to the passing scenery.

"I have such respect for you, that you turned out the way you did—coming from him," he says. "He was so different the last time I was here. That visit was an aberration. I was wrong to see it as a breakthrough. Today, even his love felt manipulative. The only person who mattered to Voldemars was Voldemars. Your mother was right. He hasn't changed."

"I agree," I say. "And the love he expressed—sometimes, he said the right words, but afterward, I felt drained. It was the strangest experience. I got angry all over again."

"I can understand," Jonah says. "I was angry, too. I wanted to run out of that house."

Heading back toward LA, we stop at Torrey Pines beach, an

expansive stretch of ocean and cliffs, not far from Del Mar. It's already dark, but I don't care. I need to clear my head, to let the crashing waves drown out thoughts from the day. So, with the sound of my voice swallowed by the ocean roar, I scream and move freely, pacing, then dancing, on the empty beach. I punch out an unseen opponent. Contained no longer, I unchain myself. Finally, I return to Jonah's cradling arms and cry.

The next day, I come down with a flu-like virus, the second illness I've had since reconnecting with my father less than two months earlier. As I lie in bed guzzling Echinacea to help my immune system, two voices cry out in me. A child voice tells me she's still desperate even for the subatomic chance that someday her father's true love will reveal itself to her. She believes only it can seamlessly forge together the broken pieces of her—as her father used to forge pieces of steel at the mill.

The other voice belongs to the woman in me who refuses to go on experiencing the rawness she feels whenever relating to her father—helping him stuff grief, telling him everything will be okay, when she wants to choke him. She can't stand him being in her life another minute without retribution, without accountability, without reparation, without some compensation to her. She demands that he grieve not only for his wife, but for what he did to me.

"Stay," says the child. "I can survive. I've learned from generations of survivors."

"Leave for good," screams the woman. "He's abusing us all over again— raping us emotionally. He'll never admit what he did. In one moment when he feared he'd be alone, he talked about the past. But that door has closed. And he now sees he won't be alone. Margo's family is there. Judy. His swimming buddies. His minister. Potential new wives. How many would even look at him if he admitted he was a child molester?"

The child and woman are silent now. I imagine inviting them into my arms, pull the blanket up around my neck and shoulders, and hug them both.

I realize I had to play out this scenario with my father—for myself. Otherwise, I would always have wondered what would have happened if I'd faced him. I would have wished I'd taken the chance to speak my truth as I looked into his eyes. I would have hoped the opening in my heart would have opened his heart enough for him to admit and atone for what he did. But it didn't. It won't. And I finally comprehend that the most loving and healing next step I can take is to walk away, bow out of this fledgling reconciliation—before I further damage myself.

For the next two weeks, I avoid talking to my father, using the illness as an excuse. I recoup and sit with the truth that has emerged. I also don't want to hit my father with this decision the week after his wife died or during the holidays. So a few days into the new year, I call and tell him I can't see or talk to him anymore unless I can freely discuss the past. He becomes hysterical, begs me not to do this, screams that I'm killing him. And for the first time in my life, I sit up straight in the chair at my desk, and I raise my voice, too, screaming as loud as my father.

"Don't get excited," he screams, interrupting. "Don't raise your voice at me."

"Don't you censor me," I cut right back in, my voice out-louding his. "Not ever again. Do you hear? I can get excited any time I want. You can't threaten me anymore with your panic attacks or breakdowns. *I'm* not responsible for them. *You are.*"

And that's it. In one instant, he stops ranting and speaks in a completely calm voice. Just like that, he turns it off. He moves into talking about the past again. He tells me quietly that if he hit me when I was a child, in the way that my mother and I said, he doesn't remember, but he deeply apologizes. With regard to the "other thing," though, he says it can't be. He begs for my forgiveness.

But even thinking the words, "I forgive you," makes me gag. *No way.* Thirty whole seconds of apology for only one part of the hurt he inflicted—and he's not even really admitting that.

He says "if" he did it.

"Is that it?" he says. "Can we forget it? Have we talked about the past enough?"

"I hear your apology, but truly, it's only the beginning for me," I say.

He starts crying and ranting again. "Now, I not only have to get over losing my wife, but my daughter, too. It will be even longer now before I can talk about the past. How can you hurt me this way? Don't do this. I beg you."

I cry out, "I hurt, too. You're not the only one in pain. Imagine how deep my pain is for me to say these things."

As soon as I escalate, he calms down again. One minute, panic. The next, a level voice. "This is the worst time in my life—and you do this."

"I've been through the worst seven years of my life dealing with incest and CFS," I say, my voice still raised. "I've spent most of my adult life trying to heal childhood abuse. So I ask right back, how could you do that to me?"

"I've nothing more to say," he says. "How do we leave it? I guess I'll let you know if I can talk about the past. But it will be a long time. Years, if ever. I'm an old man; I can't take this. That first day, I thought we resolved everything. I thought we were happy. I marked the calendar and made it our day."

"We only talked for half an hour," I say, still emotional, but lowering my voice. "Only a start."

"I have an idea. Why don't you just call every month or two? Ask your old dad how he is and tell him how you are."

"That's taking care of you, not me" I say, wrung out now, my energy crashing. "I won't do that to myself."

"But I'm not asking for anything," he says. "I only want to be able to say my daughter lives nearby, and we see each other. Now I can only say my daughter lives here, but doesn't want to see me."

Right, I think. *You're only asking for one little piece of my soul. Then another. And another.* I tell him I need to hang up, wish him—and myself—healing.

And that's that. I hang up shaking, wounded by the intensity of the conversation—but also amazed. I survived. I'm in my own apartment. Jonah waits in the living room. I never have to hear my father's voice again.

But I still feel incomplete. For eternity, my father could say he was sorry for beating me. Yet without admitting he sexually abused me, too, that apology doesn't mean much. As part of a final conversation, I want to demand that admission. I don't care that he'll never give it to me. I call him back. One ring, two, three, ten rings. "Admit you molested me. How could you do that to me? How could you do that to your own daughter?" I scream at the ringing phone again and again. Around ring 40, I hang up. Enraged, I pound my fists on a sturdy floor pillow imagining it's him. I smash it against the wall again and again. Over the next days, I dial his number again and again, each call letting the phone ring dozens of times. My father never answers.

———

May 25, 1993

Sue Colin's desk is laid out with Native American power objects. Ceremonial feathers. Rocks. Carvings. Totems. A pipe. A rattle. A pouch. Her small womb-like cave of an office is dimly lit. On its walls hang a decorated cradleboard for a papoose, a woven blanket, an eagle painting, and a poster of a butterfly—a monarch—her symbol for transformation.

The poster reminds me of a monarch butterfly I recently saw during a walk in a canyon park. Worn out after the episode with my father, I had been spending part of most days over these last several months seeking the renewal of nature in parks near the ocean and in the canyons around Los Angeles. Solitary respites from the crowded city. Not knowing what else to do, I sat, walked, and drank in rich color as the hillsides gradually turned green from winter rains and filled up with the yellow mustard flowers and orange poppies of spring. I took off my shoes and put my feet on the firm earth. I lay down, face against the grass, and drifted in the scent of fresh new growth.

When I closed my eyes to meditate, I imagined Mother

Earth, the Divine Mother of us all, rising up and holding me. I saw myself extending my roots deep into her and grounding my center into the heart of the world. My own heart opened in response to her healing renewal. And the cords of emotion that had wrapped around and bound my heart since the meetings with my father unraveled and dropped away.

My face pressed against her soft bosom. I cried with grief over what would never be. With her oak trees and gnarled pieces of lichen-covered driftwood as my audience, I expressed my anger and disappointment about what had passed. When I felt spent, I took naps on the cool earth and let the warmth of the sun caress my face and arms.

One day, I saw a monarch butterfly. Wings wet, caught in the water, she was drowning in a pond. I rescued her, but instead of flying away, she rested on my finger. I imagined she stayed because she wanted to, not because her wings were too wet to fly. Walking the length of the trail and back with her on my finger, I sent her messages of gratitude and love for coming into my life. When I returned to the pool where I had saved her, she took off and flew.

I remembered that after my maternal grandmother died, my mother believed my grandmother had transformed into a butterfly and appeared in that form to visit her. I wondered if that monarch butterfly was my grandmother, come to offer encouragement and thanks from my ancestors' lineage of women for the healing and personal transformation I was doing for myself, and in some way, for them, too, during this time. Perhaps she had come to remind me that I had been rescued from the pond just like the butterfly—in part, by my very own choices and responses to life—and that one day soon I would fly again.

Now, looking at the butterfly poster in Sue's office, I hope that the work we're about to do together will be the next step in the transformation that will free me to take flight for myself—and my ancestors.

"I believe you will become what's known among Native Americans as a wounded healer," Sue says. Sue is a psychologist and shaman, trained in the Native American tradition.

"Wounded healers are individuals who go through major challenges like illness, disability, or tragedy. They heal their bodies, minds, and spirits and learn compassion for their own suffering and the suffering of others in the process. Then, they become shamans—or another type of healer—and pass on healing to others. To my mind, the illness and abuse are serving as your shamanic initiation for becoming a wounded healer."

"That's certainly a more affirming way of looking at this journey than calling it chronic illness and sexual abuse," I say.

"The Native Americans also believe that when one part of our community is sick and out of balance, or when one part heals, we are all affected," she says. "So even now, while you're still dealing with CFS, know that any healing work you do on yourself brings healing to the larger human family."

That resonates with what other healing practitioners have told me, too. They've said the work I do, along with the work other people with serious illnesses do to heal, has a ripple effect. As I clear pain and suffering from my physical and emotional body, it ripples out, and in this way I help clear it from the body of the world, and from my own ancestral lineage.

Sue will be guiding me through a Native American shamanic healing practice known as soul retrieval. It's based on the belief that at certain challenging points in our lives—trauma, divorce, death, abuse, loss—a piece of our soul leaves the body and escapes to another realm of existence. In the case of sexual abuse, the perpetrator might steal a part of the victim's soul during the abuse. Any number of soul parts lost reduces energy and vitality, but multiple missing pieces can result in serious illness.

During soul retrieval, a shaman travels to the other realms to bring back the lost soul parts. Afterward, the person integrates the energy of the recovered portions and experiences some form of healing of the mind, body, and spirit.

We have already done two preparatory sessions to cover personal history and lay the groundwork before the soul retrieval. "One word before you do this," Sue had said the first time we met. "Make sure you're truly ready to change your life. I don't know anyone who hasn't experienced radical shifts after a soul retrieval—often unexpected ones."

I believe this. My friend, who'd referred me to Sue, had done a soul retrieval herself. Soon afterward, she'd broken up a verbally abusive relationship and climbed Mount Whitney, the tallest mountain in the lower 48 states. But even more than my friend's story, I'd had a dream that foreshadowed major change. The night before my first appointment with Sue, I dreamt I was in a school classroom with a woman who was teaching me about shamanism. When I met Sue in the lush garden outside her office the next day, my heart began to pound. The tender smile, the sensitive brown eyes, the thick, shoulder-length, dark hair. I had already seen her. Sue was the woman from my dream.

This hadn't been my first prescient dream. Over the course of my life, I'd experienced a few. But each time, they amazed me. And they always signaled a life-altering event—the death of someone I knew, a physical move, a significant meeting with a person.

This third time Sue and I meet, we do the soul retrieval. She is attired in a full, long black skirt and a black T-shirt, belt buckle, and jewelry with boldly colored Native American designs. Before starting, she smudges me with sage, fanning it over me three times with the feathers, to cleanse and purify my energy field. She spreads out a black, turquoise, and white Native American blanket, and asks me to lie on it.

She begins by singing her personal song of power, then lies next to me so our shoulders, arms, legs and feet touch on one side. She puts on headphones to listen to a tape of drumming for shamanic journeying. The drumming, she explains, will help take her into an altered state of consciousness. I can only hear the softest pulsing of the beat escaping from the headphones. I remain still and silent while she journeys with her power animal. Native Americans believe every person has one or more power animals who serve as allies and teachers. She had already taught me how to journey and meet mine, too, in one of our previous sessions.

Breathing deeply, I close my eyes, feel myself connecting

to Sue. I call on Archangel Raphael, Mother Earth, my power animal, and other spirit and animal guides I've worked with to join us. After a few minutes of lying quietly, meditating in the dim light of the small room, I sense several soul pieces beckoning in the distance—scattered like seeds by the wind in realms beyond the earthly dimension—unable to land and take root.

I see a bubble floating toward me. Peering at me from inside are a three-, a seven-, and a 15-year-old. Soon, to my astonishment, I'll discover these are in fact the ages of three of the four soul parts that return.

After half an hour, Sue gets up and blows the returning soul parts into my head and heart. She shakes her rattle all around me to seal them in, then relates her experience. "First, I was drawn to an ether world of no substance, no ground on which to stand. There, I saw a happy, spirited, but lonely, three-year-old. This soul part fled when she was first overwhelmed by the sexual abuse." The child reached out to be picked up and then nestled quickly in Sue's arms. "I ask each soul piece if she will return with me, because each must choose for herself," Sue explains. "Sometimes, I need to persuade the piece to come back, but this little one wanted right away to become part of you again."

Next, Sue journeyed to the cave of the lost children, a dark, sad place full of children who've been cast away. "When I called out your name, a seven-year-old girl emerged from behind a rock, and I thought, *She looks like an angel.* She had such a bright light in a land devoid of light. Her father cast her away there. She was so relieved to be brought into the light again. She vomited all the fear and secrets she'd swallowed in her life and created her own ritual, burying what emerged in the ground where Mother Earth could cleanse and transform it. Then, she raised her face to the sun and sounded out her voice which had been silent for a very long time."

I listen closely, tears welling up for what the seven-year-old had endured, noting that this was the part of me who left when the abuse escalated. The seven-year-old agreed to return, too.

After that, Sue saw an image of a teenager, sleeping in the back of a car. "A hellish vacation I took with my parents to California the summer before tenth grade," I say immediately. "They were fighting constantly. I slept most of the time to escape."

"I also saw her in school," Sue said. "She was 15, shy, beautiful. In the other realm though, she was chained by her father. He came toward me as a monster. I called a second, strong power animal to help me rescue her."

Sue tells me how she cut the chains with a sword of light while the power animals kept my father at bay. She and the teenager quickly flew to the safe place where the other soul pieces waited. This part agreed to return under one condition. "That Vita never allow anyone to hurt me like that again." Sue assured her, and the three soul pieces hugged and wrapped their arms around each other.

Sue had one more stop—this one in the realm of the night sky. The last soul part was an adult, a 28 year old. She was a warrior woman—powerful—and wore a shield that represented her courage. It turned into a mirror when her father came close to her. It threw his own reflection and negative energy back at him, sent him reeling backwards across the cosmos, powerless over her. "This protective part of you, that knows how to reflect back, has been lost for a long time," Sue says. "She also loved to dance and had wings that let her fly when she leapt into the air. With her shield, she was safe anywhere. But for some reason, you cast her out. Her strength and protectiveness became lost in your life."

As Sue speaks of the warrioress, I recall that I'd been studying creative movement at that age in New York City. It opened up in me a spontaneity, joy, and freedom like nothing I'd ever experienced. The dancing—and the therapy I was doing—freed up another part, too. During that period, I started writing creatively, something I'd felt called to do since childhood. I first wrote performance poetry about healing family wounds and claiming one's voice. But even though this writing made me happier than anything else and inspired me to become a free-lance writer, I had abruptly set it aside to focus more on commercial writing projects. These projects paid the bills, but they no longer came from the deepest part of me. I felt like I'd lost a part of myself that I'd only recently recovered. When I tried to return to the creative writing, I couldn't. I felt blocked.

It's this energy of creativity I most associate with the warrior soul part. As I wonder to myself why she split off, I have an insight. Tapping into the creative source of my writing, I had begun to open the portal to the unconscious that would eventually reveal the abuse memories. At the time, I must not have felt ready or safe enough to do that.

The warrior soul part agreed to come back, too, Sue says. And so, the foursome returned home.

"It's time now to be a warrioress yourself," Sue says. "To live knowing you can take care of yourself. With that shield, nobody will mess with you. It protects your whole body and all your soul parts. It's time to be in the light. Let it out and let it shine. No more darkness in the way. It's *always* been there, by the way, that light. "Welcome home," she says to me and to my soul parts.

I feel the soul parts and I unite as one being, exploding into a whirlpool tidal wave of light. I know that, together, we can dance and stumble and crawl and fly through it all.

⁓

The first week after the soul retrieval feels a bit like I gave birth to quadruplets inside my body. Each one is as needy as baby birds in a nest vying for the food their parents bring, hungry for recognition and demanding attention. When I come to Sue for a follow-up session, she suggests I ask each day what they need. She also suggests I encourage them to share what their greatest heart's desires were—the desires that were thwarted when they left, but which now can be met. The first time I ask this in meditation, the seven-year-old soul part comes forward. I imagine her outside my body on a pillow in front of me and invite her to express her heart's desire.

"I want for you to write our story of the past," she says. "The other soul parts want this, too." As she speaks, I know more than anything else, I, the adult, want to do this. Over the years since

I remembered, before I even reconnected to the warrioress part of me, the pull to write about this history has been increasingly tugging at me. But while I've journaled about my process of healing the abuse, writing more extensively about it still seems overwhelming and exposing.

"Just imagine yourself channeling the soul parts," Sue suggests when I tell her. "Don't try to figure out now whether this writing is only for you or for publication. Do it any way it wants to come out. Let these parts, who've been silenced for so long, speak through you. Create the space for this writing, an hour a day, even if you decide that you're the only one who'll ever see it."

She also gives me guidance on the writing process. "Before writing, meditate and call in your power animal and spirit guides to help you," says Sue. "Whenever the writing becomes painful or difficult, turn it over to them and request their assistance. They'll support you."

The next day, my energy level increases significantly for the first time in months.

—⁓—

The night before I begin writing, I have a lucid dream—in which I realize I'm dreaming while still in the dream state.

My maternal grandmother, who is dead in real life, stands on the stairs leading to the basement. She looks like she did in her mid-sixties—the age she was when in real time I was 11 and stopped the sexual abuse. In the dream, I am an adult, and I decide to give her a hug, thinking I'll feel her love. Instead, I feel strangely cold.

"What's your message?" I ask, drawing back from her. "Why have you come to my dream?"

"Stay out of the sun," she says. Then everything fades to darkness.

When I wake up, I realize this message is my grandmother reminding me of the dangers my ancestors faced if they dared speak out during centuries of oppression. Death. Deportation. Imprisonment. Better to remain hidden in the dark, be quiet, than take the chance of facing consequences like these. *Stay out of the sun*, my grandmother warns, trying to protect me.

Yet in the light of day, sitting on a grassy lawn surrounded by trees in a Santa Monica Canyon park, with my journal on my lap, I cannot heed her call for safety. I need to be outside in the sun—for her, my maternal grandmother, for my mother, for all the women of my family who come before and after me. I bring the darkness up from the basement into the light of healing truth. I say in my own loud, clear voice to all that jeopardized and stopped my ancestors' voices—the political oppression, the abuse, the displacement from their homes and their homeland, the threat of imprisonment and death—"No more."

Not surprisingly, the seven-year-old, the one who first knew at that very age she wanted to be a writer, the one who has instigated this process, emerges from the soul parts, asking to tell her story before the others. I remember that her favorite books at that age were *Black Beauty* and *Lassie*—stories of brave, loyal, beautiful animals who survived many hardships and abusive humans before finally returning to loving environments and peace. The child in me starts with these words:

I am seven years old, and it fits that the fog rolls in as I begin to tell my story. That's what happened in my life. A fog rolled in, a thick cloud that disconnected me from my life and pummeled me into darkness.

Thus I set in motion the process that becomes her story, the other soul parts' stories, and several years later, my own story of incest and abuse as I tell it in this book.

The Miracle of Grace

Sue was right. She said to be ready for major changes after soul retrieval. First comes the writing. Two months later, Jonah and I decide to move to a small Southern Oregon town, full of culture and heart, after a visit there. We've felt called to live closer to nature, away from urban pollution, pace and stress. Several health practitioners have also suggested a move like this might help heal the CFS.

"Your work here is done," says Sue, when I tell her we are moving. "You needed to be in Southern California near your father to heal your past with him. Now, you've healed as much as you can here. You and Jonah are ready for a new place to live."

Three years pass. Our new home is a small Victorian on a tree-lined street within walking distance of the center of town. It's set in an expansive valley surrounded by mountains. There, I continue to ride the blessings of breakthroughs in healing my body, life, and spirit and to work with a growing number of helpers—human and divine—on this journey.

One in particular, Suzanna Solomon, becomes my soul sister and spiritual mentor. During regular meditations and individual sessions, she supports me in learning how to consistently connect and co-create with my divine self and the angels, ascended master teachers and spirit guides available to help all of us. She helps me deepen the faith and fortitude required to continue to face and transcend the challenges of illness and abuse.

But, in early 1996—in spite of all my work to heal, transform, forgive, and move on—the unthinkable happens. The CFS takes a shocking and disheartening turn for the worse. I relapse so badly I can only concentrate 15 minutes at a time and have to stop working even part-time again. In some ways, I've slid all the way back to the first days of CFS. In others, I feel even worse. I can't read a book. Many days, I can't put my thoughts together to remember what I did an hour or a day earlier. I come to dread when friends call to ask, "What have you been up to?"

I'm so environmentally sensitive I mostly stay inside with air filters or air-conditioning running, even in cold weather. In the car, I use recycled air and close the windows, or I get so brain-fogged I can't drive. I develop such severe food sensitivities that I'm on a highly restrictive diet and have reactions to nutritional supplements that are supposed to help me. I am envious of every person walking down the street, thinking, *If only you knew how lucky you are simply to take a stroll or order a sandwich.*

For several months, I make slow headway following the comprehensive integrative alternative medical program of a renowned CFS physician, Majid Ali, whom I'd traveled across the country to see. Yet in May 1998, one and one-half years into the relapse, four and one-half years after I move to Southern Oregon, allergy season hits full force, and the CFS symptoms become even more pronounced. I am concerned about my emotional state. It's breaking down like my body is. My will to endure, to live, is flagging. I am profoundly tired of dealing with CFS and the abuse issues that still come up when I do emotional or spiritual healing work.

It's an intense time for the earth as well. After a second exceptionally wet and dreary winter, Southern Oregon has had rain every day for weeks. Everywhere I go, people ask, "When will we see the sun again?" At the same time, fires rage over hundreds of thousands of acres in Mexico and Florida. Are these signs of the earth changes, the dark times before the new dawning that so many seers and Native American elders have been predicting? Is this the earth crying out ever more loudly for us to change our ways? Is this my soul crying out for me to change in some way I'm not hearing?

May 23, 1998

The First Night of Darkness

One night, I fall to the lowest emotional point I've hit on this journey through illness and abuse. I've had an allergic reaction to a drug I've taken to help alleviate some of the CFS symptoms. It's made me so sluggish I slur words and have to fight losing what little consciousness I have. The resulting imbalance has also plunged me into a depression like none I've ever experienced. Even though I've stopped taking the drug, it won't pass out of my system for 24 hours.

Sitting in the dark in my small wood-paneled living room in Oregon, on the same rust-colored couch that's seen me through so many crises and processes, I cry uncontrollably. I don't want the light on. I don't want Jonah in my presence to hold or comfort me. I don't want consolation. I want to die. I wouldn't take my own life, but pray adamantly and loudly for God to take it.

"I've had it, Mother-Father God, Divine Creation," I say. "I've done the best I could in this body, and I know I've done great. I may have screwed up royally at times. But I've learned so much, opened, and loved. Now, I have no more to give this life. No more, do you hear? I've given everything to healing, and I have nothing left. So please, I beg you. Take me. I want death and I want it now." I tell God I'm sorry I haven't found the total healing I worked so hard for. I ask God to help Jonah forgive me too, for no longer praying to heal and live, but to die. The quality of my life has sunk too low. After 12 1/2 years, no matter how fully I've accepted and embraced life, no matter how much I love Jonah, my mother, my friends, I've been in pain too long, faced too many setbacks, too many new challenges. I can't go on. I give up.

After crying and praying from these depths, expending the little energy I have on pleas for a quick and painless death, I feel spent. I stare into the darkness, depleted. The only hope I have left is for God to answer this death prayer. Eventually, even that hope disappears, and my mind goes blank. Time passes, and a story my friend Shayne once told me insinuates itself into the blankness. One night, in the throes of pain about a terrible relationship he was in, he went out onto his land in the Oregon countryside and asked God to help him die. He told God he had lived a good and full life. Now, this relationship was so painful he had nothing to live for anymore. He was ready to die. Two weeks later, he was diagnosed with terminal colon cancer. It had metastasized. He was told he had six months to live. Quickly, he ended his relationship and moved to Southern California to receive treatment at City of Hope. Within a few months there, he reconnected with his first wife. They had married when they were young and had divorced after a few years. But in the midst of his life-and-death struggle, they fell deeply in love again and remarried. Now, all he wanted to do was live a long life so they could be together. He did indeed live for another two beautiful years before he died.

That story drops into the emptiness in my mind like a slap in the face. Perhaps this friend already had cancer when he sent out that call to God. Still, it was a chilling reminder that even when things seem like they'll never get better, if we can hang on, miracles and tender healings can and do happen. Even the worst pains can fall away and lead to heart openings, new purpose, and joy.

I grow uneasy about the certitude of my first prayer. And, from somewhere deeper than the prayer for death, I reach in and pull out a new one. I pray that those thousands of cells inside me—which, I've read, can at any instant transmute and turn cancerous, grow a tumor, or create some other untimely death—don't.

I have enough strength to cancel the first prayers, but not to transform the pain inside. I sink again. This time into shame that I'd pray my life away. Shame that I've experienced miracles, and can still whine about anything. Shame that I've been sick for so long. Shame that I've gotten better, but relapsed. I am so ashamed I don't want to be seen. Not by anyone. I'm ashamed that instead of this person of goodness and love and light I've worked so hard to be, I'm flawed, miserable, angry, full of judgment and doubt. I'm ashamed that since this relapse, I haven't been able to accept what is, surrender one smidgen to the Divine or give up wanting to control things myself.

But somehow, yet again, something shifts, and the shame drops away. While my mind races from one thought to the next, it no longer latches onto them. It is past midnight. I get out my journal, turn on the light, and write about this experience. I write with passion and feeling. Gradually, the emotional pendulum slows its swing. I fall asleep curled up on the couch, holding the journal against my heart.

⁓

May 30, 1998

The Second Night of Darkness

One week later, still in the process of trying to balance the extremes released during the night of darkness, I wake up at 4 a.m. and can't fall asleep again. I'm more anxious than I've ever felt—this time, without even a drug reaction to blame. I imagine plunging into the fear, embracing it. This is what I write:

I awaken at 4 a.m. with such anxiety I cannot contain it. I try to hold it in some way, but I cannot live with this much anxiety. Hell, I don't want to live this way. At the same time, I no longer want to be rid of it, give it away to God or anybody else, push it away, take a pill for it, contain it.

So I dive in and let it carry me. As I plunge, I see myself screaming and tearing at my clothes and hair. I am running through my normally peaceful, small town streets. "I'm a failure," I scream. "I am crazy and nothing in my life has turned out how I planned. I am a wild woman. I am not this nice tidy package of spiritual, loving, aware woman I'd like you to believe I am. I am a holy mess of a woman with twigs in my matted hair and mud smeared all over my breasts and belly. I am torn and tattered, and I have allowed life to split me open—wide, wide open. I don't fit into the containers of houses and jobs and roles anymore.

"I come from the nunnery of the wild woman, where instead of dressing in a nun's habit, I wear patched-together garment rags as sack cloth. Each day, instead of doing good works, I rip and wring apart these rags until they lay shredded upon the cool stone floors of my black hole sanctuary. Instead of praying, I foam at the mouth, and rant and scream the cries of cosmic pain and rage and laughter. Every night, as people sleep, I piece my bits of rags together, and start the process over again.

"But I can't rest in the nunnery anymore. It's no longer my place, and it's too damn hard to hide who I am from the world. So I run through the streets and let everyone see the woolly wildness of me, the holy mess of me, the rough edges of me. The failures and mistakes and sticky illness and deadness and abuse stuff and can't-get-it-together-in-my-life-ness of me. And I get it over with—let it all out, confess, so that all the citizens of my community will know at once who I am."

I stop running when I reach the home of a couple I recently met. Their lives are full of good values and responsible action and positive manifestation and service and ease. They are spiritually and emotionally and physically beautiful. I want them to like me, and I fear that if they see that my life has not come in a proper package and is an outer-world disaster, they won't. But I stand outside their house anyway, let them see me screaming and ranting and foaming and tearing away.

"You are contributing, in the name of love, to the planet," I yell, my voice carrying loud and true. "Yet I contribute, too. I live on the rough edges for you. The Christians say that Jesus died for our sins. Well, God knows, I'm not Jesus, but I live on the rough edges, ride the rough-edged path so others don't have to. And I'll have you know it's a razor-sharp edge that cuts right into my butt, slices right on through me, if I sit down too hard or rest too long. I am learning my way this time around, just as you are learning yours. We're all *experiencing a part of the picture and the whole picture at the same time. Even if I don't have to stay on this edge forever, I do need to learn it. And I need to express it.*

"This is who I am. This is the truth of me. I am a mass of rough edges. I am healing a split so wide you can't see the other side and witnessing that split from the inside out. I don't really live in this peaceful town, even though I have an address here. Now out of the nunnery, I go to live in the underworld with my mate, where we gnaw and tear at the bones of the dead. We serve each other up gourmet dishes of our dark sides—taking the ingredients from every void and abyss of the sooty center of the earth. We make dishes like salad drenched with tears of pain and sadness, duck à la rage, wild woman fried rice, blood-and-guts sausage stuffing, and fear à la mode."

But there is more. Another side. As I stand, my heart and body split wide open for everyone to see, I let this couple and the townspeople see that this messiness is also my path to love and Spirit. I allow them to see that love. Experience its bounty. The love pours out of me without me doing anything. So much I can't contain it. Love for me and my wild woman, savage though she may be. I love that I have ridden her edges and survived, and I tenderly recognize that those edges are my roots of passion and creation. Tears of sweet love pour out, a nectar of compassion for myself, love and compassion for my mate and friends, for my mother and family, for the couple, but much broader. I have so much love to share in this moment, so much love that comes from having touched the deep pits and warts and oozing sores of me. This love extends to the whole world, to every living being on this planet, to every saint and murderer and all the muddling souls in between, to each plant and animal and mineral and water source, to air and fire, to every atom and quark and infinite space in between, and beyond space, to every spirit being.

I am the love that arises from being all of it—the love and the hate, and the never-ending pain and joy and sadness of it. I no longer concern myself with the couple's acceptance or rejection. It's no longer an issue. I love and appreciate myself for being who I am. I have no more shame or self-judgment in this moment of pure love. It's not even about forgiving myself or my father or anyone else anymore. It is purely and simply about acceptance of myself and my tumble of a path, which in the world's eyes may look like a bust, and may never be a perfectly plotted life. But it's perfect for me.

After I finish, anxiety replaced by calm, I fall asleep and dream about a new friend of mine, a psychic reader and wise woman named Lucy Wade Barth.

In the dream, Lucy and Michael, her significant other, are hosting a party. While there, I begin to feel extremely tired and look for Jonah to tell him I'm leaving. I start to faint, stumble to where he stands, and crash onto a couch beside him. My heart pounds loud and fast. A huge energy fills me and blasts out through my chest. I realize I am entering a shamanic healing passage, but I need help to move with the energy. I whisper, "Get Lucy," as the energy explodes, builds, and explodes again in waves.

Waking up with my heart pounding wildly, I decide to tell Lucy about the dream the next weekend at a meditation group we both attend. My hope is she'll help me move some energy.

June 8, 1998

The Truth About Grace and Vulnerability

Even before I see Lucy, shifts begin. The wild woman writing purges something in me. Somehow, this little piece that poured through me non-stop in 20 minutes, this gift from the divine muses, infuses my will to live with new life force. Once more, I'm ready to take whatever steps I can to heal myself.

I'm able to accept what is now—to breathe with it, even if that includes breathing with it in an achy, barely functioning body—and to stop running away simply because a feeling or situation is uncomfortable, or triggers old stuff. This kind of acceptance isn't about resigning myself to a lifetime of illness or leftover wounds. Instead, it's about dropping the *judgments* around what I'm experiencing—no longer calling myself, or what's going on, "good" or "bad," "safe" or "unsafe." It's trusting the process I'm in is leading me to the truth, to a deeper recognition of my authenticity. It's about surrendering to the divine wisdom that says I chose to come here, to live this—in this body, in this life, no matter how difficult my circumstances have been. It's also about trusting that even if events don't always turn out as planned, I have the resources inside me to face everything I need to face. I have infinite divine assistance available to help me.

⌒

When I see Lucy, she relates she, too, dreamt about us working together. In her dream, we play with a huge ball of light. I stick my hands right into it and toss it to her. She catches it and tosses it back to me.

We agree to meet at her house and "play." Lucy, an intelligent, generous woman with strawberry-blond chin-length hair, wears a neutral-colored, short-sleeved shirt that hangs loose out over her jeans. She suggests we begin with a Tarot card reading—the method she most often uses to work energetically with people. We sit on the hardwood floor of a big room overlooking the Cascade Mountains. She spreads a large number of cards in front of us. As soon as she speaks, I experience the same shift in energy I've felt in the past in readings when psychics are on track with their perceptions.

When she opens up the reading for questions, I ask why, even though I've worked so hard on myself, I'm still not cured physically. "In my own experience, you don't have to work for divine grace in order to get it," says Lucy. "You don't have to prove yourself. God just gives it to you. In fact, most of the people I know who experience grace don't deserve it at all. It simply happens."

An *a-ha* moment sneaks in and strikes me like a bowling ball against ten pins. A beautiful strike. I realize I've always thought I need to prove myself and work hard in order to deserve and receive God's grace—and God's love. At that moment, I understand on a deep level that this is not the case. Not for me or anyone else.

Grace comes in many forms. Sometimes, it's purely a matter of perception. On a recent day when I was feeling sorry for myself, these words came in meditation: "God showers you with grace, and all you see is rain." I realized I had so much to be grateful for in my life, so much grace even in the difficult lessons. Yet in that moment, I had only been focused on what was wrong—the physical ailments and left-over abuse issues.

I ask Lucy about the push-pull I feel about writing the story of this healing journey. Since putting aside the stories of the soul parts, I've resisted a persistent inner voice that's been guiding me to put the story into book form. Part of what holds me back, I tell her, is an aspect of the abuse wounding I haven't been able to work through yet—the fear that if I put my vulnerability out in the world, I'll be abused again.

"Vulnerability is your strength," Lucy answers without hesitation. "I remember something else from my dream. You had light all around you. You were saying, 'I can't get it to come out.' But I saw the light as *already* present, already out. There's a real strength in your vulnerability. Your writing is a way of expressing vulnerability as strength. Some part of you, though, keeps realigning vulnerability with weakness, and shies away."

"It was that vulnerable person who was manipulated and raped by her father," I say.

"But if your vulnerability now—away from your father—is where your real strength lies, and you move away from it, how can you heal and get well?" she asks. "By blocking off this vulnerability, you're paying a price—and blocking what I think is a real power for your healing. It's like you're sacrificing yourself. If I were to give you homework, I would say, run the phrase, 'Vulnerability is my strength' over and over and over again in your mind, until you see the pure naked truth of it."

"Try telling that to my ego. It says, 'Yeah, right. See ya.'" I say.

"That may be true, but this phrase is the key to what you want to do," says Lucy. "It's the strongest reminder word-wise I can find for you. You're a bright person, and have good mental skills. But they're blocking you from truly, dynamically healing—by just a little. Such a little. If we trick your ego into thinking it's safe, it'll release and let you go, so you truly can be safe. You're actually safer with only vibration, divine energy, to support you. But sometimes it's hard to take that leap of faith."

"It has been for me, that's for sure," I say. "In my head, I know the answers: *Give up control*—which we don't have anyway. *Surrender to Spirit*, because that's where the real safety lies. *Trust Spirit is always there* and *we're never alone*. But I get stuck asking, 'Where the hell was Spirit when I was being abused?' Even though, rationally, I know It was there then, too."

"Wherever It was, you survived. So someplace It was connected to your survival," she says. "And where was the ego? It was connected to your survival, too. And why are you still working with them now? Because acknowledging both ego and Spirit, loving them both, working with them both—that's connected to your survival. In my opinion, though, this illness goes beyond personal concerns. Maybe there's a positive reason for all this. Some grace in all of it. Something you don't understand or comprehend, rather than something that's wrong with you or needs to be fixed."

That night after working with Lucy, I have this dream:

I am back in Ohio, on the land that used to be my father's but isn't anymore. The house he built has been torn down, and a beautiful new house, owned by a woman with long, dark-blond hair and bangs (like me), stands in its place. It has stucco siding and dark wood trim, like houses I used to love growing up, which were located in the well-to-do, older communities in Cleveland. The ceilings of the house are high. It has lots of angles, living areas, and different-shaped towers.

I'm with a male friend, and tell him I'm nervous my father is going to return. I don't fully trust he's gone. But he is. Even without knowing for certain, though, I take a chance and begin to circle around the house. I stop in the yard and call out as loudly as I can, "I claim my power." At first, my voice comes out haltingly, tentatively. Quickly, it builds in strength and volume. "I claim my power. . .I claim my power." Over and over again, until my voice is full and strong. I wake up.

June 11, 1998

The Hidden Root

A few days later, I have a "failed" root canal re-treated. The endodontist found a "hidden" root that wasn't worked on eight years earlier during the first root canal I had on this tooth. For more than a year, he says, it has been releasing the toxins of a "silent" infection into my head and body.

June 12, 1998

A Lesson in Miracle Thinking

The next day, Friday, feeling better than I have in months, Jonah and I decide to celebrate. Ordinarily, we go to movies on Friday nights. But we've already been invited to a housewarming party that lasts until 7 p.m. All the movies we wanted to see start earlier.

That series of circumstances leads me to browse the entertainment section of the newspaper. I see an ad for a workshop entitled *Shifting into Miracle Thinking* presented by two healers passing through town. It's being sponsored at a local Grange Hall by a church I'm not familiar with. So I don't know if the healers come out of New Thought spiritual philosophy or if they're from the many Fundamentalist Christian groups who pass through Southern Oregon for revival meetings. But considering what's been going on these last weeks, I don't care. Divine healing energy is divine healing energy, regardless of the source. I feel strongly motivated to go.

The Grange Hall is a nondescript gray building I've driven past many times without ever noticing. The inside is equally plain—one large room with a sliding vinyl divider that cuts it in half, brown vinyl floor covering, white walls and two paintings of nature scenes. About 40 people sit in neatly lined rows of folding chairs.

I arrive with a "come what may" attitude, without expectations. I'm so happy to be feeling a little better today, I'm able to be neutral. I'd like to have a healing, but I'm not attached either way. I'm simply showing up as a "good faith" action to express that I'm participating in life and healing again. In some way, I feel like I died that night of the drug reaction, had my own version of a near-death experience and life review. I returned with nothing to lose. I'm simply here, all splayed open, present and accounted for.

The healers, Margaret and David Hiller, are also psychologists and spiritual counselors, who work using New Thought philosophy. They talk about the miracles they've witnessed. Margaret, who has chin length auburn hair and a slight Southern accent, wears a flowing orange-gold top and skirt. She tells stories about cancer disappearing, a child's club foot straightening, and a newborn growing a missing heart chamber. She describes dental healings—where people grew back teeth that had been lost, teeth were straightened without braces, and mercury fillings changed to gold.

David has shoulder-length, gray-white hair, a beard, and a moustache; he wears a purple shirt with jeans. He emphasizes the importance of moving out of "surviv-al" mode and into "thrive-al." Here, you live fully and bless each moment regardless of your life circumstances. He guides us through a meditation and group exercises. Both Margaret and David smile easily and speak with warmth and enthusiasm. By the time we take a break, I am inspired to sign up for the longer workshop the Hillers will be holding on Sunday, and for one of the private sessions they offer the next day. Since I don't have a strong pull to one over the other, I toss a coin about whom to see. The coin says Margaret.

⌒

June 13, 1998

The Commitment

During the second half of the Hillers' seminar, my recently treated tooth starts to hurt. It feels like it's becoming infected.

While I hate the idea of taking antibiotics, the pain increases so much through the night I have little choice. The next morning, on my way to a 10 a.m. healing session with Margaret, I stop off at the drug store to pick up the antibiotics and painkillers prescribed by the endodontist. The effects of the antibiotics won't kick in, he says, for 36 to 48 hours.

Margaret greets me at the door with a big smile and leads me into her friend's home office at the house where she's staying. The space is small, only big enough for a desk and the two chairs on which we sit facing each other. It looks out on a back-yard garden and patio, filled with flowers, plants, and rocks.

We begin with a prayer to set the intention for healing. I tell her an abbreviated version of my story, mention the wild woman writing and the calling I feel to write about healing the abuse.

"When do you feel the most alive?" she asks.

"When I write something from the fullness of my being," I say.

"Then, you must write," she says.

"Do you think I should write my own story, even though I'm resisting it?" I ask.

"What I would prescribe is to write your own story from your soul," she says. "Not from the little perspective of 'we've got to get the perpetrator,' but from the larger perspective of 'This can't go on—the way we abuse each other and ourselves—even those of us who weren't sexually molested. This is how I was hurt. This is how my father was hurt. It's got to stop. And, for me, it stops here.'"

This woman doesn't mess around, I think to myself, a bit amazed at the forcefulness with which she tells me this. But she's not saying anything that I or other people haven't repeat-edly said to me over the last few years. Only this time, I'm really listening—without the walls and defenses and rationalizations I usually use with myself, or the bargaining chits I toss out to Great Spirit about what I might do instead. Her words have the effect of a whiff of smelling salts shocking me out of a dead faint. They blow me awake. I listen as if I'm glued to my seat with my mouth taped shut.

"You've been holding on to your story, because it'll be forgotten otherwise," she says with compassion in her voice. "You need to get it out of you, and writing it seems to be your means of expression. In my humble opinion, you made a soul choice before you were ever born to live this story for a higher purpose. Now you make the choice to tell it or not. What's the worst that can happen?"

"I'm afraid I'll die if I tell this," I say.

"Okay, so you die," she says. "People kill you for telling the story. You can be reborn. They can't really kill you."

"I'm also afraid I'll personally hurt people if I come out fully and tell this," I say. "That if I take my power like this, I'll end up being like my father."

"You are a wise, beautiful woman. You chose to come into the world this way to help heal humanity, not to end up like your father," she says. "Go beyond shame, judgment, fear, pain, or hurt. Just tell the truth. Something larger than you wants to speak through you. It wants to tell this story from that bigger perspective of you healing yourself. I believe this story can end up contributing to healing others, too."

"But it's so painful," I say. "How can that be healing to anyone?"

"It can," she says. "It's the ripple effect. Every story of abuse needs to be told so it isn't repeated, so humanity learns. Elie Wiesel, the writer who came out of the concentration camps, said, 'Forgive, but never forget.'"

"Even if I did decide to write from this perspective, right now, I can't do much of anything," I say, my tooth throbbing more as we speak. "How can I write a book when I only have 15 minutes of concentration at a time?"

Margaret suggests that to start, I do at least one thing daily that is larger than my human limitations. If I can't write, I can sing or speak words out loud instead. I can paint or dance naked in the moonlight. The point is to do something out of character, that's not controlled or protected or limited.

"Your father said, 'I control you,'" says Margaret. "Now, you control yourself. You mentioned periods in the past when you burst forth in your life, then seemed to clamp down on yourself again. That takes tremendous energy. It's time to get beyond 'protecting' yourself by not writing or speaking this story. How long will you sacrifice yourself in order to protect yourself?"

Her words shoot right down to my cells. The longing I've stuffed to write this story, despite the difficult nature of the subject matter, fills me. And there's that dreaded word, *sacrifice*, again. Lucy had used it, too, only a few days earlier. *By continually blocking off this vulnerability, you're paying a price—and blocking what I think is a real power for your healing. It's like you're sacrificing yourself*, she had said.

"Do this for yourself," Margaret says. "The people in your life will love you whether or not you do it. But this is your healing. Your life force. Stop holding onto it and protecting yourself from an evil world. I believe the illness is tied into this. If writing the story does in fact kill you, so be it. That's better than living this way. Right now, you're killing yourself, which is no better than killing others or being killed by others. Speak the truth. Feel the fear. Ride it out. Feel the pain. *Ride it out.*"

Her words shock me. I've never thought of how holding back the story is a way of abusing myself. In this self-repression, which continues even without my father's physical presence, I abuse myself like my father abused me. Before, only my tooth hurt. Now, I feel nauseous as well. *Is this supposed to be a healing?*

"This story goes beyond sexual abuse," she says. "It's part of all the harm we do to each other, to ourselves and to the planet. We need to hold hands with all the abusers and the abused and envision healing for all of us. Rudolf Steiner said that as the world story comes out, we must hold it in love, contain it in love."

Margaret stands up and asks if she can gently run her hands over my head and shoulders and give me a healing. I agree. As she does, she also prays. We both hold the vision that I make the decision to let it all out, rather than hold it in, and tell this story.

After the session, I drive home feeling both agitated and filled with a peace I haven't experienced in years, maybe never.

When I tell Jonah what I got from Margaret about writing the book and that I'm going to do it, he says, "You must do it now." He pauses and asks, "What if you don't have a physical healing after you write it?"

"It doesn't matter," I answer. "I'll know I've healed on the deepest level anyway."

"That's the answer I wanted to hear," he says, explaining that, over the years, he has seen me do many things, hoping they'd result in a physical healing, and come away disappointed when it didn't occur.

⌒

That night, though, the struggle about whether or not to tell the story re-emerges. It seems to play itself out in the pain of the tooth infection, not quelled by the painkillers. Each hour it intensifies, it comes to symbolize all the pain of those years I cried out to express myself, to release the pain of my past, but couldn't or didn't. The pain seems to be pounding, "No more. No more," in my head. The pain also seems associated with anger—that I feel relentlessly compelled to tell this difficult story.

At 2 a.m., I call the hospital emergency room to find out how much I can safely increase the dosage of painkillers. After taking the additional pills, I end up writing in my journal about my internal struggle. Those words eventually become the first chapter of this book. When I finish, I know unequivocally that I choose to write my story, no matter what—even if that means I have to share the deep vulnerability that is supposedly my strength. Even if I have to do it only 15 minutes a day.

⌒

June 14, 1998

Healing Grace

The next afternoon, after taking many drugs and getting no sleep at all, my tooth still throbs. The CFS symptoms are so flared I can barely sit up in the car as Jonah drives us to the workshop. I need a miracle to get through the event, let alone participate. At the worst, I decide I'll lie on the floor, out of the way somewhere, and hope to pick up any stray healing energies. I still don't have expectations I'll have an actual healing. My brain is too fogged and preoccupied with the physical symptoms. But I know in some visceral way I *must* get to that workshop. God knows, I need any kind of healing today, with 12 more hours to go before the antibiotics kick in.

In the car, I grow increasingly nauseous, because I took my last batch of painkillers and antibiotics on an empty stomach. When we arrive, I stumble out of the car and teeter like a drunk on a binge to the back of the building. There, I proceed to vomit five times in full view of several people arriving to take the workshop. Jonah comes over, holds me by the arm, and we walk inside.

Today, the folding chairs are arranged in a large oval, and about 30 people have come to participate. As the Hillers begin speaking, I barely see them or hear anything they say. Most of my energy goes into staying upright in the chair. They ask us to pair off for an exercise in energetically healing each other. Jonah does the healing for me first in the hopes that the energy I receive will give me enough of a boost to at least remain sitting with the group. David leads the exercise. "I call forth to the infilling of the light of the Divine," he says. For the first time since I've arrived, I become aware of his words and try to imagine doing what he says. "I call forth to a perfect circle of love and light to surround us. I call forth to the holy healing breath of God to breathe through us, and I call forth to the Holy Spirit to fill our hearts and souls with Divine Love."

He envisions that the healing energy each person is sharing goes exactly where it's needed, and suggests that the healers stroke the heads and shoulders of the people being healed—like Margaret had done for me in our private session. They're also to whisper supporting, loving, healing words to those receiving healing.

Jonah stands behind me, lightly strokes my head, hair, shoulders, and whispers, "You are a star child manifesting the fullness of your being." I feel loving, warm energy coming to me from his hands. Yet when he finishes, I still desperately want to lie down. When we're asked to switch roles, I tell Jonah to work with someone else, because I'm too weak. He lets Margaret know what's happening. She pairs him up with another person, then comes over to me. I ask if I can lie down for the rest of the workshop.

"Is it okay if I give you another healing first?" she asks. I nod my head, and she takes her place behind me. As David speaks again, she strokes my head and shoulders. Instantly, I feel electric charges of energy igniting my hair and head. Margaret whispers words into my ear, but the only ones I remember are: *"I don't mean to disrespect you, but the message I am getting to tell you is that you can let go of the CFS right now and release the illness. You don't need it to protect you anymore."*

At that moment, everything shifts. Strong waves of energy start to course through my body. I feel like I'm liquefying. I want to scream out like the Wicked Witch of the West after she's doused with water, "Oh, I'm melting, I'm melting." Instead, sobs overtake me. My shoulders heave up and down. It's not me that's melting, but the disease in my body. I literally experience it melting away, peeling away in layers. Margaret continues to stroke my shoulders, and I keep repeating, *I can indeed let go of this now. I am letting go of the illness.* I feel this is so—down to the core of my being.

A miracle is taking place. I'm going the entire way to healing. All movement forward, no holding back, no turning down the volume, no little voice of doubt. Five short minutes in real time. Yet I know my life has been transformed. Grace has irrationally and beautifully descended into my life—not caring whether or not I deserve it or have used up my quota of miracles.

I can't stop crying, and Margaret tells me to let it out. "Tears are holy water," she says. "Honor them." But she is unaware of the full extent of the miracle that is transpiring. She returns to her place next to David to continue the workshop. They ask people to share their experiences. After a couple of people do, I raise my hand, wanting to share why I'm sitting in the circle bawling. Between sobs, I blurt out that I'm truly in the middle of a miraculous healing. David immediately asks everyone in the circle to hold hands.

"What is it you most want in this instant?" he asks.

"A-a-a com-plete a-and t-to-tal heal-ing," I blubber through my tears.

"Okay. Let's all hold hands for a minute or two and hold that intention with you," he says. "We ask that a complete and total healing take place for you right this moment." He continues to talk, but as everyone in the room connects hands in the circle and holds this shared intention, my entire focus turns to the increased energy I feel surging through me.

Afterward, the sobs subside, and everyone else gets up to take a break. Jonah and I remain seated. But this time, it's by choice, rather than necessity. I feel totally energized and healthy, the only remnant of illness a dull ache in my jaw from the tooth infection.

"Your soul is on your face again, like it was when you had the healing with Raphael," Jonah says, and he beams as he holds my hands. No one else can possibly know what he and I have been through—individually and together—over the dozen years I've been dealing with CFS, sexual abuse, and the other challenges we have faced. Twenty minutes earlier, I had been so sick I couldn't sit up. Now, he and I know I'm completely healed.

During the break, I sign up for a second private session—with David this time because Margaret is completely booked.

As soon as I do, I'm once again overwhelmed by nausea, even worse than the first time. I rush to the lavatory, throw open the toilet lid and vomit over and over again. This vomiting is unlike any I've ever experienced. No matter how close to the toilet bowl I bend my head, the force of the expulsion is so great, I am wrenched back. I projectile vomit all over the room, like children sometimes do. I feel like Linda Blair in the movie, *The Exorcist*, as she receives the exorcism from the priest. Seven times, I vomit this way, until yellow green bile vomit covers the blue vinyl floor and white walls. As best as I can, I clean it up, and rejoin the group, which has reconvened into a circle. Everyone stands to receive individual healings from Margaret and David and to support the energy for each person getting a healing.

During this final process, Margaret and David once again stroke everyone's head and shoulders. They anoint everyone's forehead with water mixed with dirt from the famous Catholic chapel in Chimayo, New Mexico, and the well-known natural location of a Mother Mary sighting—Congers, Georgia—places where miraculous healings occur regularly. In my dress pocket that day, I also happen to have a packet of soil from Chimayo. My mother sent it to me earlier that year. Every day since, I'd carried it in the pocket of whatever I was wearing.

Afterward, I mention the vomiting to David, and he says, "That's part of the healing. You're purging all the remnants of the illness and of the past."

———

At home, I lie down for two hours, and the waves of energy start again. I get up long enough to eat some steamed vegetables in broth, put on a pair of pajamas and climb into the downstairs bed in my office to sleep. I know I need to sleep alone. Throughout the night, I drift in and out of consciousness, awakened again and again by the energy waves. Repeatedly, they build to a crescendo and release into a sense of calm and peace. As the night proceeds, the energy intensifies. My heart pounds for several hours. I feel hot tingling all over my body. It's as if I've become the primal fire of me, the yin-yang-chi-storm-roar-creative-cocktail-kundalini-snake of me. As certain as I am I experienced a healing earlier, I'm now uncertain about whether I will live through the night or burn up from the inside out. I *do* still know, though, that if I die, I die healed.

At one point, my cat, Orianna, who usually sleeps with me, comes into the room and stands next to the bed looking up at me. She scans the length of my body from the top of my head to the tip of my toes. Once, twice. Three times. I watch her head moving back and forth, her eyes widening, her ears lying back flat along her head. She races out of the room and doesn't return the entire night.

But I don't burn up as I open more and more to ride the fire within. Instead, the fire and I build a ring of divine protection from which the light in me can safely shine forth—in healing and transmutation. As I ride this grace, I see that the power of the fire burns with the essence of love and divine co-creation— not destruction. And I see that my power—and the power of the visions come back from the past for divine restoration and recording—come from that same essence. I can trust that now. I can trust myself.

June 15, 1998

Soul Choice and a Word on Forgiveness

By early morning, the intensity of the healing fire evens out. Filled with the grace of Divine Love, I sink into the all-encompassing embrace of Divine Mother-Father. I remember that during the workshop, David said, "If we only knew how much we're loved by God. . ." In this moment, I *do* know. I know, too, that understanding I'm loved in this way, letting myself experience this love, I can do anything I need to do. I can co-create a healing. I can create a circle of love around me. I can write my story, and express my truth.

I stay in bed until noon, lolling in the arms of the Divine and meditating in great gratitude for what has transpired. I get the message to stay with the healing experience and away from electrical power sources as much as possible during the week— not to use the phone, watch television, or listen to music. I'm also not to socialize. But in a day or so, I ask Jonah to call my mother and some of our closest friends to tell them what's going on, and to ask them to pray for a moment each day that week for my complete and total healing—like the workshop group had done.

Later that afternoon, in a session with David in the same office space in which I'd worked with Margaret, I connect more deeply with the knowing that I made the soul choice—before I ever came into this body—to experience everything from the incest to the

CFS. The purpose was to know each challenge from the inside out. To share it with people in the hopes that it would serve as a catalyst for their own spiritual evolution and transformation.

He suggests that as part of the healing process, I do a ceremony in which I bless everything that's led me to this point, including sending blessings and healing to my earthly father. I'm finally ready to take this step. I am still no saint. I may feel ready to forgive, but I don't forget. Forgiveness is an ongoing process for me. If my father calls me tomorrow and once more tries to minimize what he did or get back into my life, I might be angry all over again and have to forgive him another 70 x 7 times. I also know that I don't ever want to be in my father's verbal or physical presence again.

But even as a flawed, now healthy human being, mucking her way along the forgiveness path, I recognize in this moment that, in the truest sense, I'm not now nor was I ever my father's victim. For reasons beyond my human comprehension, I chose this challenging path of spiritual evolution to heal myself on a very deep level, and to reverberate that healing out in a way that might touch the lives of others. I accept this and with that acceptance, I realize the anger I carried about the abuse and the CFS is gone.

"One more thing," David says. "Celebrate this return to nature, the mother of us all, and fill your house with flowers. Keep it filled with flowers to remind yourself of where you've been and how far you've come with this healing."

And I do. I go home and fill my house with vases of flowers. Roses cut from our yard. Fragrant peonies and colorful African daisies from a flower shop. Flowers in every room. And, for the first time in a year and a half, I am not overwhelmed by allergies.

June 17, 1998

Gratitude, Blessing and Other Wonders

On Wednesday, three days after the healing, it's time to test its full extent. For the first time in over a year, I go to a nearby park, and walk its hiking trails. The rains have finally stopped. The sky is deep blue, the creek is running high. The trees, shrubs, and grasses are iridescent green. Flowers bloom everywhere. To anyone witnessing me, I'm just another hiker enjoying this pristine day. But going into the park is for me the equivalent of entering the belly of the beast—in my case, a hotbed of concentrated pollen. This walk represents another rite of passage, too. It's the first time I've hiked the length of the trail since a major flood changed its landscape in January 1997, a few weeks before the CFS relapse . I have come alone, wanting to do this by myself. I'm dressed for celebration—wearing red shoes, a rainbow-colored shirt, purple pants, purple hat, and lavender sunglasses.

As I walk along, nervous about putting the healing to the test, I'm aware I remain symptom-free. I feel present, clear-headed, grounded, and energized. While some of the trail remains washed away and hasn't been rebuilt, I'm amazed at how much nature has already renewed itself—despite the flood wounding. Both the park and I are healed.

I remember what Margaret said about doing something out of character. So, letting the energy of joy take me, I walk a little, then spin round and round down the path. I skip like a child and click my heels together mid-air, first to one side and then the other. I feel like Gene Kelly in *Singin' in the Rain* and dance the dance of Vita, the dance of life.

I break out into a spontaneous song of thanks, voicing my gratitude for every living thing. Tears of joy stream down my face for the ability to do these simple acts of walking and playing and singing in the park—acts I will never take for granted again. I walk with more confidence now, stopping often to breathe in deeply the smells of flowers, leaves, cedar, pine, fir, the wood chips on the path, the freshness of the air—scents which for so many months had affected me like poison gas.

All the way up the trail and back again, my thank you song unfurls to include gratitude to everyone who has walked with me on this path of healing, first to the blessed ones like Jonah, my mother, my friends, family, counselors, spirit teachers, physicians, and authors of inspirational books and personal healing stories. Then my thankfulness extends to the people who tested me and pushed me beyond what I felt I could bear—most notably my father. I give thanks for the grace of each moment and event of my life, even the CFS and the abuse—the stern teachers who taught me and opened me up so much. I know that every single one has served a higher purpose I don't always recognize at the time. And, I give thanks to the Great Spirit for being with me and loving me for eternity.

I hear a distinct voice in my head. *Go to the reservoir. This is where you're meant to send blessings and healing to your father like David suggested. It's time.* So after walking nearly two miles, I return to my car and drive more deeply into the park to the reservoir. My heart pounds again. No more perfect spot exists for this blessing.

I was last here in December 1996, after receiving a Christmas card from my father, his first correspondence since I told him I couldn't speak to him unless we could discuss the past. The card was one created for a child, with a sweet painting of a little girl, a syrupy greeting and a handwritten note saying, "Call and let me know how you are. Love, your dad." In a releasing ceremony on a gray, drizzly winter day, I had burned the card at the reservoir's edge, and had later written back to him, saying not to contact me again unless it was to admit the incest.

Today, nothing will intrude on the elation I feel. On my way, I'm inspired to stop and pick a blue cornflower to use as part of the blessing ceremony. I also pick up a piece of driftwood—my father and I both loved and collected driftwood, which he used to decorate our house—and a sparkling, rough-edged, multi-colored stone. The reservoir, reflecting the blue sky and the tall Douglas firs, cedars, and pines surrounding it, isn't open to swimmers yet. At noon, the picnic area around it is completely empty. The creek, high with rainwater and snowmelt, rushes into the reservoir with a strong current. It separates the spot where I originally burned the card from the rest of the shore, turning it into a small island.

Knowing I need to go there anyway, I remove my red leather tennis shoes—my old ruby slippers. I had bought them before leaving New York and was wearing them the day I met Jonah, a *Wizard of Oz* aficionado. Hiking my jeans up to my knees, I cross the rushing water slowly, surprised by its strong pull and icy coldness. I slip a couple of times on the stones and mud, but make it to the other side unscathed. Placing the driftwood and stone side by side at the water's edge, I imagine the driftwood represents my father and the stone symbolizes me. I invoke divine light to surround and protect us all and lovingly call on my divine guides to join us, too. In addition to the white horse, my power animal, and the Archangel Raphael, I've met and worked with other guides over the years, too.

I speak words of forgiveness from my heart, send blessings of God's love, and pray for my father's healing, pray for the healing of that which is so lost and wounded inside him that he could repeatedly rape his own child. Compassion rising up in me—for him and for me—I pray the entire situation be healed in the light of love, the cycle of abuse stopped in our family and the whole human family, forever.

In the same waters where I placed the ashes of the Christmas card I burned 19 months earlier, I now place the blue cornflower, releasing it into the current. Asking that as I release this flower, I release my father from my cells, I cut all negative ties to him, and put the past behind me. Throwing the flower, I aim for the center of the current and watch the flower follow a zigzag path. At one point, the blossom gets swept up by a second current that carries it toward the left shore. I'm afraid it will get stuck there. Instead, as it slows down in calmer waters, yet another current sweeps it up and carries it back into the center of the reservoir. It bobs along toward a waterfall created by a stone dam, which will carry it into the creek. I watch it for a time, then lose sight of its small blue head. When I think it's too far away to see or assume it has sunk, the sun once more catches the tiny blue blossom in its light. It's heading not for the waterfall, but off course again to the left toward a stone wall. *At least it made it to the other side,* I think, releasing my expectation that the flower will go down the waterfall to freedom. And, boom, another current picks it up. Eventually it does ride over the waterfall into the creek and is gone from my sight forever.

I give thanks, thinking I'm complete, but a voice in my head pipes up. *Your mother is a part of this family, too. She needs to be included in this ceremony.* Not one to argue with this voice of guidance, right there on my little island, I spot a smooth, delicate pink stone that reminds me of my mother, so I place it next to the driftwood and the multi-colored rock. I send my mother blessings, too, and ask the Divine for a complete healing of her life and anything concerning the abuse. Empathizing with all she has seen and experienced, and, with warmth radiating through my heart, I give great thanks for the repeated help she gave me over the years, the tangible display of her love, and the healing she's done with me regarding the past.

A little blue butterfly flies around my bare feet. I've been experiencing my grandmother's presence often over the last weeks in meditations, wonder if she's come to me in this form, as she has in the past for my mother and me. I invite her to join with us also to represent the healing of all the generations of my family, the healing of their legacy of abuse. Amazingly, the butterfly lands on the earth right by the stones and driftwood directly in front of me.

An image appears to me now of my father, my mother, and me, standing in a circle holding hands. Generations of family, angels, and divine guides surround us. As I recognize the soul choice all the ancestors made to come together to perform this particular family dance, I honor the profundity of the roles we played in helping each other evolve and experience even more compassion and forgiveness for all the pain of the drama called abuse.

I see my parents and me turn into radiant balls of light, first three individual balls, and then merging into one. We expand and unite with everything around us, becoming one with the universe. A moment later, we're one big ball of light, laughing, heading over the waterfall after the cornflower, riding the rapids and currents of the creek. Our masks gone, we've returned to our divine states, beyond our human drama.

Leaving the stones and wood in place, I once more cross the creek. The pale-blue butterfly continues to hover around my feet, accompanying me for a time. I pick up my red shoes and walk barefoot back to the car, feeling the energy of divine Mother Earth stretching from her core up through my feet and throughout my body. Near the gate, the butterfly leaves. The moment I reach the entrance to the reservoir, which had remained empty for my entire ceremony, three carloads of adults and children pull up and begin piling out chairs and picnic baskets. As I leave, they enter the gateway.

Somehow I'm not quite complete. The same voice that guided this ceremony now tells me to turn on the radio. A new song starts to play, as perfectly timed as if I'd popped my own cassette into my tape deck. I listen to the lyrics to see what message they hold. A soulful song by Al Green says you can have anything you want. You can fulfill your heart's desires. But you've got to give it everything. "Love is what you need" is the refrain, and the name of the song is *Give it Everything*.

I get the clear message once more that I've come back from illness and childhood wounding to give my life everything. To live full out in love. Ultimately, love is the main lesson I've learned from all my experiences. It is what I am, what I need, and the greatest gift I give, too.

My heart brimming with gratitude, I sing along with full voice, not caring I'm massacring the lyrics. While I drive, I bounce up and down, dance at the wheel. I can't believe how this journey has unfolded, and how perfect this song is at its conclusion.

In truth, one piece of this perfect picture won't reveal itself for a few more years. On June 14th that year as I celebrate the anniversary of my healing and the completion of the main draft of this book, I'll find out from my mother that June 14th is another significant anniversary for our family. June 14th, 1941, tens of thousands of Latvians, including several members of my family, were sent to Siberia as part of Stalin's purge of that country. In some way I'll never understand, my healing was for those family members, too. My writer self couldn't have made it up any better.

June 28, 1998

An Answered Prayer

Two weeks later, the healing feeling more integrated into my body and energy field, I wake up early one morning and contemplate once more what I've learned over the years of dealing with CFS and abuse. I pick up my journal to write down the essential lessons that come to me. As fast as I can get them on paper, I effortlessly compile a list of 100 teachings—on loving and being loved, acceptance, surrender, compassion, forgiveness, courage, faith, giving and receiving, gratitude, and the power of connection to Spirit.

This list will become the foundation for another miracle, one that unfolds in tandem with the physical healing.

It actually had begun a few months earlier. In February, I woke up in the middle of the night, overwhelmed with angst about my future. I wondered how many more people facing illness and other challenges were awake, alone, in pain. I prayed fervently that night for help and direction for all of us. To my astonishment, when I finished, this prayer was immediately answered with the idea to create a nonprofit website with articles, inspirational stories, and self-help tools to help people face and transform the adversity in their lives. At the time, I expanded the concept enough—with Jonah's brainstorming help—to receive the promise of funding from a private donor. But I was dealing with so many CFS symptoms that I couldn't go on with the project. I had put it on hold indefinitely. Interestingly enough, one week before the physical healing, I had simply let it go.

Now the list of lessons that came to me in this meditation becomes the listing of categories I will cover on the website. In

July, I will call my donor and reactivate the project. By December, I'll receive nonprofit status. One year later, in January of the new millennium, I will go online with Lifechallenges.org, the CyberCenter for Living Creatively with Life's Challenges. It will eventually reach people in 87 countries around the world.

⌣

July 5, 1998

The Gift

Before I even start working in earnest again on the website, however, three weeks after my healing, I begin the process of writing this book—just as I had committed to do 12 hours before the miracle healing occurred. Completing the main draft of the book will take four more years, but anytime I feel lost or overwhelmed, all I have to do is think back to the healing to know the universe wants this story told, and I am its conduit.

I wear a present Jonah gave me on that first day I started writing—a pink T-shirt with blue lettering that says: *Vita is a Miracle.*

When he went to pick it up at noon after ordering it two hours earlier, the store owners told him, "As soon as we finished the shirt, the electrical circuitry blew. It was the one shirt we did today. We only stayed open to give it to you because you wanted it as soon as possible. Now, we're closing up and going home."

"I chose pink and blue to symbolize the balance of male and female," Jonah tells me. "And for the newborn part of you. Besides, 'You're now in the pink, and the T-shirt represents that, too." We laugh together, as we have so many times throughout these years despite the trials. But the laughter is lighter today. I give him a long, deeply felt hug.

That night, I get into bed still wearing the T-shirt, my hands touching the felt letters on my chest. *Vita is a miracle, indeed,* I think to myself, and soon fall asleep.

⌣

Acknowledgements

This book birthed its way into being with the grace of many helpers, supporters, friends and guides. I bless and thank you all, named and unnamed.

To my soulmate, Jonah Blue. Thank you for living this with me, loving me, bearing witness, sharing tender hugs, and for helping me both find the larger perspective and hold space for the vulnerable humanness. For your inspired editing and clear vision through the revisions of this manuscript and the suggestions that helped me trust that "less is more." For sharing your own luminous creativity and process. Our love makes it all possible and worthwhile.

To my mother. Thank you for your love and support in my life and for this book. Your courage, resilience, joy of living, beautiful spirit, and willingness to show up inspire me daily.

To my partners in YES, my incredible publishers, Irene Kai and David Wick. Thank you for saying yes to the voice of the soul, for your expansive vision, boundless passion, and the grace and wisdom you bring to every moment and detail of our publishing journey. I honor all levels of our remarkable connection.

To Suzanna Solomon. Thank you, precious soul friend, for the inspired co-creation over the years that helped me open to grace in all forms. For holding the vision of this book's creation and manifestation. For your wisdom, compassion, meditations and soul work, and most of all, your loving friendship through the tests and joys.

To Mary Rexford. Thank you for the generous and courageous editing that guided me to the revisions I needed to make to focus, hone and complete this book and for your insightful feedback in the two writer's groups we shared. Thank you for the blessings of friendship, heart, laughter, conversations about writing and craft, and for your own beautiful writing.

To Margaret Hiller and David Hiller. Thank you for encouraging me to honor *Riding Grace* as a soul path and valuable "healing story" and especially for riding grace with me and supporting my "shift into miracle thinking."

To Molly Tinsley. Thank you for generously reading the draft of this manuscript, for the heartfelt hug and words, "You must write this." They cleared a path when I'd lost my way. Your class and editing helped me deepen as a writer and get back in touch with why I love writing.

To Sue Colin. Thank you for the transformative healing work we did together, and the encouragement both to write the story of the soul—and move to the Northwest.

To Majid Ali, MD. Thank you for your inspired vision of healing, for hope and for a brilliant healing approach to chronic illness. For the support, dedication and spiritual perspective you provide for me and so many people facing serious illness.

To my writer's groups through the years: Lori Henriksen, Jane Maitland-Ghoulson, Shoshana Alexander, Jodine Turner, Maggie McLaughlin and Tiziana DeRovere. Thank you for your insight, encouragement, the gift of reading many drafts and holding the vision with me as I birth this book. Your writing inspires me daily. Thanks to Dia Paxton, Asha, Rita Grauer, Terrie Claflin, Pat Morrison, Nancy Bloom, Lisa Bleier, Deborah Davis, Sierra Faith. Thanks to Te Zins for the photograph.

Thanks for traveling "the front lines" with me and loving me: Tresha Cuomo, Rob Geier, Lorena Gonda, Steven Kiralla, Evy Mcpherson, Larry Newman, Barbara Rayliss, Bridget Reynolds, Michael Arnold, L.A. Seva group, Cori Bishop, Lucy Wade Barth, Michael Barth, Kathleen Conroy, Herb and Elaine Hyman, Jacqueline Kramer, Mort Smith, Karen Joy and Michael Turley, Swami Ty, Orianna, Rosedale, and my maternal family.

Thanks to Jerry Terranova, Ashalyn, Franci Prowse, Tim Ray, Don DeLong, Eetla, George Weinberger, Johanna Wright, Jan Baker, Sara Owen, Robin Rose, Gloria Schwartz.

Thanks to the authors and movie makers whose work inspired and transformed me and the mind-body-spirit pioneers who expanded my perceptions of miracles and healing. Thanks to Mother Earth for soul nourishment.

To my muse, guides, angels, the Divine—thank you for your wisdom, guidance, blessings, grace and love.

Alissa Lukara is a writer and president of Lifechallenges.org, a nonprofit website of articles, self help tools, and inspirational stories, which help people around the world creatively face and transcend adversity. Lifechallenges.org has been featured in popular books, magazines and websites, including those of the American Chronic Pain Assn., the Assn. for Humanistic Psychology, the Muscular Dystrophy Assn., and the Art and Healing Network. She produces and hosts the television program, "Transcending Life Challenges," and lives in Southern Oregon with her life partner, Jonah, and her cat, Orianna.